THE
SUPERGLUE
SANDWICH

THE
SUPERGLUE
SANDWICH

BY DAVID LAWRENCE

**Clues for people who are
stuck for an answer**

Scripture Union
130 City Road, London EC1V 2NJ

© David Lawrence 1993

First published 1993. Reprinted 1994

ISBN 0 86201 892 7

Cover design and illustration by Ross Advertising & Design Limited,
Book illustrations by Neil Pinchbeck.

British Library Cataloguing-in-Publication Data
A catalogue record for this book is available from the British Library.

Phototypeset by Intype, London.

Printed and bound in Great Britain by Cox & Wyman Ltd, Reading, Berkshire.

This book is dedicated to

my Mum
(who taught me how to iron shirts)
and Dad
(who taught me how to wear a tea-cosy on my head)

Special thanks to

my wonderful wife, Myrtle, for being herself

the community at Stanton House
and Douglas and Beryl Munns for giving
me sanctuary whilst writing this book

Alison Barr, Jo Bicknell and the many
other Scripture Union staff who have
had a hand in its production and distribution

the members of Christ the Rock
Christian Fellowship, Yate, who have put up
with me for the past ten years

Mark, Andrew and Tim,
education advisors and proof readers

Introducing . . . The Superglue Sandwich

Biting into a Superglue Sandwich would be a truly gob-stopping experience. One bite and that'd be it – lips stuck together, tongue fixed to the roof of your mouth and it's off to Casualty you go.

Although no one would ever really make or eat a Superglue Sandwich, lots of people do have that gummed-lips-and-stuck-tongue experience. It usually comes just after some clever clogs has asked a difficult question about God or Jesus or the Bible or being a Christian or . . .

You know the sort of thing. 'You don't read the Bible do you? That stuff has all just been made up, hasn't it?' Now you know that you should be able to give a well-reasoned answer, but your lips refuse to open and your tongue refuses to budge. You have just been fed a Superglue Sandwich! !

This book tries to get between the crusts of several Superglue Sandwiches (see the Contents page for a full menu) and give you some of the answers to those mouth-stopping questions.

You don't have to read the chapters in any particular order. The first bit of each chapter is supposed to be funny so, in the interests of safety, please don't read it whilst fire-eating, performing brain surgery or landing a jumbo jet. Thank you. You have been warned.

Contents

Testing, testing!

In every class, there are a few people who are determined to muck about, whatever the lesson and whoever the teacher. And there's perhaps no lesson which gives these characters more scope for releasing their misplaced energy than Science. Anyone who can cause a disturbance in a lesson like English, where we only use paper and pens, will have a riot of a time with acid, electricity, bunsen burners and a wide range of other chemicals. The whole thing seems set up for disaster, and it's only thanks to the patience and skill of our Science teacher, Mr Stevens, that the school isn't blown up on a regular basis.

I've thought long and hard about why Science tends to bring out the worst in people, and I've come to the conclusion that it must be something to do with the awful Smell that hangs around school science laboratories. Whatever the Smell is, it clearly acts as a stimulant to class idiots' brains, causing them to behave twice as stupidly after inhaling just one or two lungfuls.

I once decided to work out what caused the Smell and asked ten people in our class what it reminded them of. I thought that a combination of their answers might lead me to the truth. However, since their answers led me to believe that a cat wearing old football socks had rubbed Vick on itself and then laid itself down to die in a pile of rotting fish and bad eggs under the floorboards, I'm not so sure about the accuracy of my findings!

Science lessons come in two sorts – Practical Lessons where we do experiments, and Boring Lessons where we write about experiments that the school can't afford the equipment for us to do (you know, things like 'Make a working model of a nuclear power station'). Today's lesson was a Practical Lesson, and Mr Stevens had all the equipment out ready for us when we arrived.

The experiment we had to perform was to find out what sort of stuff electricity flowed through and what sort of stuff it didn't. First Mr Stevens gave us a demonstration.

'Right then, quieten down. Watch and listen carefully because you've got to do this experiment yourselves in a minute,' he explained. 'First let's look at the equipment you'll be using. Two batteries and battery holder, three lengths of wire, two small spring-loaded clips – called crocodile clips – a small light bulb and the five different kinds of material that you are experimenting with – a piece of copper, steel, wood, perspex and cardboard. Can you all see that?' he asked.

Thirty heads nodded so he continued, 'First, slide the batteries into the battery holder like this. Now take one piece of wire and attach one end of it to the positive terminal on the battery holder and put a crocodile clip on the other end, see?'

We did, so again he continued, 'Take another piece of wire and attach one end to the negative terminal on the battery holder and the other end to the light bulb holder. Finally, take the third piece of wire and join one end to the spare terminal on the light bulb holder and join the other crocodile clip to the loose end. Yes, what is it, Florence?'

Florence Torrance put her hand up to ask a question. Florence was clever but cautious. 'Please, Sir. How do we know which end of the wire to attach to the battery holder and which to the crocodile clip, Sir? Is there a right way and a wrong way?'

'Good question. No, it doesn't matter which way around the wires go. Now, as you can all see, we have two loose ends of wire with clips on. What do you think we could do with these? Yes, Brian?'

Brian Smart, not noted for his scientific knowledge, had raised his hand. He suggested, 'You could put them both in acid, Sir'.

'And what would be the point of that?' queried Mr Stevens.

'Well, Sir, it might cause a massive explosion and we could have the rest of the day off and ...' Brian was stopped in mid-sentence by the sort of look from Mr Stevens that could penetrate 10 cm of thick armour plating at 100 metres.

'Thank you, Brian, for that contribution to the furtherance of mankind's scientific knowledge. Give me your address before you leave in case you're nominated for a Nobel Prize. Now, since no one has any serious suggestions about these two loose ends of wire, I shall show you. You take one of these five pieces of material... Yes, Florence, what is it now?'

'Please, Sir. Which piece of material do you take first?'

'It really doesn't matter, Florence. Any one will do. Now, let's take this piece of copper. We attach one clip to one end of the copper and the other clip to the other end. . . Who can see what's happening?'

This was an easy question and half the class had their hands up. Somewhat unfairly, I thought, Mr Stevens asked Florence again, perhaps since she was waving her hand so hard and fast that it was in danger of detaching itself from her wrist and sailing out of the window.

'Sir, please, Sir. Which end of the copper do you put which clip on, Sir?'

Mr Stevens frowned and snapped his reply. 'Florence, it really doesn't matter. The question was, "What happens when I complete the circuit?" Andrew, you tell me.'

'The bulb lights up, Sir,' answered Andrew correctly. 'Good and what does that tell us?' asked Mr Stevens.

'Well, it tells us that the bulb isn't broken, dunnit Sir?' observed Andrew.

'Yes, yes, yes, but what does it tell us about the piece of copper?'

Everyone looked a little blank, so Mr Stevens explained that the power coming from the battery was going down the wire and clearly passing through the piece of copper in order to light up the bulb. So the illuminated bulb showed us that copper can carry an electric current.

'Now take your sets of equipment and, following my example, test the five different materials on your tray. Take careful notes of which ones carry the electric current and light the bulb and which ones do not. When you've finished testing the five given materials, test any other material of your choice. Maybe a ruler or a pencil lead will give you an unexpected result.'

We all got into our four-person project groups and began the experiment. It was about ten minutes before the Smell claimed its first victim of the day. All had been quiet(ish) when a piercing scream broke the atmosphere of studied calm. Mr Stevens erupted into action, bustling towards the scene of the cries, the tails of his white lab coat flying in his wake.

The cause of the disturbance was not hard to find. Brian Smart's group, having finished testing the five given materials, had obediently looked around for their 'own choice' of material to test. Doubtless under the influence of the Smell, they decided to test Richard Morrison's head and clipped the loose ends of their wires onto his ears. Richard's screams were due not to any excessive electric voltage flowing through his head, but rather to the excruciating pain caused by the two small crocodile clips attached to his ear lobes.

Mr Stevens unclipped Richard from his electronic earrings then rose to his full height and delivered the standard Science-teacher in-a-strop speech. You know the one, all about science labs being dangerous places full of expensive equipment and people who can't be trusted with practical work having to do writing for the rest of the term etc., etc.

The lesson concluded in a subdued fashion. The classroom was unusually quiet, in fact at times the only sound that could be heard was Richard Morrison whimpering every time he ventured to touch his crushed lobes.

By the way, the experiment proved that only the copper and steel of the given materials conducted an electric current, except in Florence's group which sadly

The cause of the disturbance was not hard to find.

worked the whole lesson with flat batteries and so concluded that nothing at all conducted electricity!

THINKY BIT

Scientific experiments are clearly very useful. The human race has discovered all kinds of stuff through scientific research that has improved life on earth for millions of people. (Scientific research has also discovered all kinds of things that has ruined life on earth for millions of people – but that's another story! !)

Under controlled conditions you can do all kinds of research to find out what things are, how they work, how to improve them, etc. Sometimes I think it would be very useful if we could put God in a science laboratory and take a good long look at him! Then when some of our friends say things like, 'Yeah, but you can't know what God's really like, can you?' or 'If God is there, why doesn't he show himself?' we wouldn't feel so superglued, but could point them to the latest scientific research into who God is and what he's like.

But that, of course, is not possible. So how can we be sure what God is like and how *can* we know him? On the surface it looks like a lost cause. Human beings trying to understand an Almighty God who can create whole universes is about as likely as an ant trying to fathom out how to programme a computer. No, we could never get hold of God and study him. He's too big and our minds (even the best of them) are too small. So what hope is there? Are our friends right to say that God is unknowable, a cosmic hide-and-seek expert who always manages to stay hidden, but leaves just enough clues lying around to show where he's been?

No, this isn't what God is like! He doesn't play hide-and-seek. It's a game he's not very good at because he *does* want people everywhere to know him and to understand what he's like. Some may ask, 'Why doesn't he give us a few more clues?' The answer to that is that he's given us the biggest clue we could wish for. The name of The Clue? It's Jesus.

Just before Jesus was arrested he had supper with his closest friends. Jesus knew he was about to be arrested and killed, and his friends were going to be left all alone, without his guidance and help. It was vital that they understood as much as possible about who he was and why he had done the things that they had seen him doing for the past three years.

So during the conversation that night Jesus tried to

impress upon them that he wasn't just a wise teacher or a kind man with magical powers, but he was actually God-in-a-body. Let's listen in to a bit of their conversation. (You can find it in John 14:7–9 *The Living Bible*.)

Jesus: 'If you had known who I am, then you would have known who my Father (God) is. From now on you know him – *and have seen him!* !'

Philip: 'Sir, show us the Father and we will be satisfied.'

Jesus: 'Don't you even yet know who I am, Philip, even after all this time I have been with you? *Anyone who has seen me has seen the Father*. So why are you asking to see him?'

Jesus was quite clear that God is knowable. Jesus claimed that by looking at his life, his friends were actually looking at a sort of acted out visual aid of what God is like. The rest of the New Testament also sees Jesus in this way. Here are some more verses on the subject:

Jesus 'reflects the brightness of God's glory and is the exact likeness of God's own being. . .'
(Hebrews 1:3)

Christ is the visible likeness of the invisible God.
(Colossians 1:15)

Now you can't get much plainer than that, can you? The '*exact* likeness of God's own being' can't possibly mean that Jesus is just a bit like God. God wants you,

16

me and everyone to know him so much that he lived on earth as a real live person.

This should really help us to know him better. You see, if we only knew that 'God is love' we might guess that it meant 'he's kind to good people' or 'he never gets angry', but when we see Jesus – God come to earth as a real live person – touching lepers and healing people who thought of themselves as his enemies, we know that God's love must be a far bigger thing than that. There are lots of things we can learn about God from looking at the life of Jesus, but here are just four to get you started.

1 *God is real*! !
This probably seems a bit basic, but it's very difficult to account for Jesus' life in any other way than that he was God. He was certainly more than just another good person. Good people don't usually have the power to calm storms by just shouting at them, and good people don't claim to be God! Mad men might, good men don't.

So, maybe he was a con man, tricking unintelligent people into following him so he could get rich at their expense. No, that's no good either because all sorts of people followed Jesus and they all had the choice as to whether to follow him or not. Furthermore, Jesus lived and died a poor man, his only possession the coat he wore. No CD collection, no country palace with swimming pool, not even a skate board, never mind a stretch limo.

So maybe ... or maybe... There are loads of 'maybes' about Jesus, but only one 'maybe' fits all the facts. This is the way that a man called Michael Green puts it in his book *You Must Be Joking*:

If you still say, 'Jesus was just a good man', I shall say, 'You must be joking'. That is the one thing he cannot be. That is the one thing the men on the spot never thought of calling him. They were terrified of him: they believed him, or they hounded him to death. But nobody . . . said of him, 'What a splendid preacher we had in the synagogue last Sabbath. You must come along and hear him some time.' Jesus does not present himself to us as the best example of the human race. . . He comes to us from beyond the human race, *as God himself*, hastening to our rescue.

2 *God cares*

Sometimes people think God is a really angry old chap, lobbing thunderbolts at people who displease him and gleefully looking forward to the day when he can lock up everyone he doesn't like very much in hell.

Even, a quick look at the life of Jesus makes it crystal clear that God isn't perpetually angry – like some heavenly Oscar the Grouch. Time and again we see that when Jesus came across needy people he cared enough to go out of his way to help them. At times he was even moved to tears by people's needs. For example, when he looked at the crowds of people swarming around him, many of whom were unwell, had no hope in life, or were worried about their uncertain future, we read that 'his heart was filled with pity for them' (Matthew 9:36).

In another place one of Jesus' good friends, a man called Lazarus, had died. When Jesus arrived at Lazarus' grave he saw Lazarus' sister, Mary, and all of Lazarus' friends still crying and deeply upset. We read that 'his heart was touched, and he was deeply moved. . . Jesus wept' (John 11: 33,35).

It's comforting to know that God cries at the hurt and pain in the world. He's not sitting on a cloud, with a couldn't-care-less attitude. His heart is touched – he cares deeply, deeply enough to ensure that one day justice will be done and all those who have caused others to suffer will pay the price for their cruelty.

3 God is powerful

It's all very well having a God who cares, but if he can't do anything then all those tears and all that compassion are nice . . . but pretty useless! However, Jesus never stopped at feelings and tears. His feelings and tears frequently moved him to do something to undo people's suffering. Jesus the Action Man must have been an awesome sight.

When the forces of nature threatened to sink the boat that Jesus and his friends were in, he didn't whip out some distress flares or ring the Galilee Coastguard on his mobile phone! No, he 'commanded the wind, "Be quiet!" and he said to the waves, "Be still!" ' (Mark 4:39). And in both cases they did what they were told!!

When some people brought a man who couldn't hear or speak, he didn't pat him on the back and tell him to 'Have a good day' – he healed him so that he could hear and talk properly (Mark 7:32–37).

Coming across a blind beggar by the road side he didn't pray that he would have a long and happy life – he healed him (Mark 8:22–25).

Jesus shows us that God is more than able to do

whatever he wants to do. Nothing in all creation is stronger than him.

4 God wants friends

Jesus recognised the fact that people were separated from God's friendship by the wrong things they said and did. He saw that people had become blinded to who God was and had lost their way in trying to be his friends.

Some of the religious people Jesus met recognised that too. But the way they dealt with it and the way Jesus dealt with it are completely different.

The religious people took the attitude that if people had done wrong and had stopped being God's friends, then God must be furious with them and would punish them for rebelling against him. The formula was simple: if you do wrong, God will clobber you; and, since everyone at some time or other had done something wrong, if God ever turned up on the scene a lot of clobbering was bound to happen!

However, Jesus gave a different picture of God's attitude to sinful people. Yes, God *did* hate sin. He hated it when people told lies and hurt each other by the things they said and did. He hated it when people ignored him and believed that they could live quite happily without him. But what he longed for most of all was not the punishment of people who had done wrong, but instead for the day when they might give up doing wrong and follow him again.

Jesus' friend John writes, 'God did not send his Son (Jesus) into the world to be its judge, but to be its saviour' and Luke tells us that Jesus said, 'My purpose is to invite sinners to turn from their sins, not to spend my time with those who think themselves already good enough'.

Isn't it great to know that God is patient with people like you and me – and our friends at school? He's not sitting in heaven gloating over a great long list of mistakes that we've made but longing for us to change our minds, and ask to be his friends. He doesn't want enemies to punish, he wants friends!

If possible God wants every single human being to stop ignoring him and become his friend. Jesus' friend Peter put it this way: 'God is patient with you, because he doesn't want anyone to be destroyed, but wants all to turn away from their sins.'

SO WHAT?

1 If your friends ever ask you how you can know what God is like, you now know that the best way to start answering them is to focus on the life of Jesus.

2 In case you ever get confused about what God is like (and just about everyone does from time to time), go back to Matthew, Mark, Luke and John and read about Jesus. Shape your ideas of God on what you see in Jesus.

3 Jesus shows us that God wants to take action to help people in need. That's also what he wants his friends (you and me) to do. If Jesus was in our school and met someone who had a problem or who didn't have many friends or who everyone else poked fun at, he wouldn't just pray for them or wish them 'A good day' – and nor should we. Jesus the Action Man not only shows us what God is like but also what God wants *us* to be like. Jesus' caring attitude would have moved him to help the person with the problem, chat to the person

with few friends or stand up for the person who was being laughed at. Do you care that much?

Tales of the unexpected

School trips come in several shapes and sizes. At the smaller end of the scale there are local trips on foot, when we have to do surveys of the local area. These are usually arranged for the wettest day of the year and involve us sitting next to a busy main road counting how many lorries, cars, motorbikes, skateboards and ox carts pass by. This information is recorded on a clip board, taken back to school and turned into graphs. It is a useful exercise but no one knows why or for whom. At the other end of the scale are the sorts of school trip which involve a coach trip and one or more members of the class being sick.

It was one of the latter sorts of trips that was proposed by Mr Grovey the Drama teacher. It was a 'cultural' trip and the day's programme consisted of a coach trip to London to visit the Natural History Museum in the morning, and the National Theatre in the afternoon, where we would be shown around and stay to watch a play in the evening. (Don't ask me

Mr Grovey had personal reasons for wanting to go there . . .

why a trip to the Natural History Museum should be
included in a trip arranged by the Drama Department
– the only reason I could think of is that some of the
exhibits in the 'Neanderthal Man' section closely
resembled Mr Grovey, so perhaps he had personal
family reasons for wanting to go there. Who knows?)

We all set off at 8.45, equipped with sandwiches, note
books and pocket money. The journey was fairly
uneventful except for Tony Peters being sick (I did warn
you that it was one of those sorts of trips!). Tony Peters'
mishap was particularly interesting since he had been
certain that if he didn't eat any food, he couldn't bring
anything up, and he'd decided to test his theory by
having no breakfast. No breakfast, that is, if you didn't

count the travel tablet that his mum forced down his throat as he left home. Now you wouldn't think anyone could manage to be sick after eating just one travel tablet, but that's exactly what Tony Peters did, reproducing his tablet at 65 miles an hour half way down the M1. (Actually if you add the speed of the pill to the speed of the coach it probably emerged at about 130 miles per hour!) Anyway, this one incident caused almost endless debate as to the relative merits of tablets, breakfasts, mothers, etc. and, thinking about it afterwards, it was quite a good job that he was sick since the resulting discussion made the journey to London seem to fly by.

The morning went quite quickly with everyone 'ooing' and 'aahing' at the exhibits at the Nat Hist Mus, and all went well until we arrived at the National Theatre for our tour. Apparently there had been some mix-up. No one knew that we were coming and all the tour guides were otherwise engaged. Mr Grovey, faced with the dilemma of what to do with thirty-five boisterous kids, thought fast. We had to go somewhere for the next four hours, it had to be indoors (it had started to rain), and it had to be free. He hit on the idea of a trip to see the delights of Harrods, London's poshest shop.

As we left the coach to enter Harrods we were given strict instructions. Don't leave the group that you have been put in. If you get lost, contact one of the store's security guards immediately and, above all, don't touch anything expensive. This last instruction was the toughest one since absolutely everything in Harrods is extremely expensive. In fact if it's not expensive they don't sell it. Anyway we entered the store, passing the doormen wearing their top hats and tail coats, and started to be impressed by the luxurious luxury of everything we could see.

I was in the group led by Mr Grovey and Ms Shore. All went well as we inspected the various departments of the shop, until we arrived at the Pet Department. On the shelves were the most amazing assortment of goodies for wealthy pets that you could imagine – gold-plated flea collars (you wouldn't think a flea could wear a collar but apparently it can), diamond-studded gerbilariums, and cut-glass goldfish bowls (especially for your cut-glass goldfish).

Standing in one corner of the department were two elderly ladies wearing fur coats. They were examining the shelves of vitamin-enriched Chihuahua food with great interest, all the while speaking in loud Harrods-type voices.

'Well, dahling, little Herbie had such a tewwible tummy-wummy after that last lot of food that I decided never again to give him anything but the vewy best that money can buy.'

Her friend replied, 'This looks vewy good. It's made by the same company that supplies the Queen's corgi food.'

Meanwhile Mr Grovey had found something rather novel. It was a clockwork spider, designed to amuse cats, I suppose, though how they were supposed to wind it up beats me! ! It consisted of a black ball of fluff about the size of a human fist with two legs which, when the thing was wound up, would rotate, moving the 'spider' across the floor.

'Go on, Sir, give it a go.'

'Certainly not, I haven't paid for it.'

'Oh, go on, Sir. It wouldn't do any harm, would it, Ms?'

Ms Shore seemed to think that a little 'go' wouldn't do any harm, and she was probaby right, but Mr

Grovey seriously overwound the thing. When he put it on the floor and let go, it shot off at the speed of light. It was only a split second before Mr Grovey set off in hot pursuit, bent double and running with arms outstretched in an attempt to scoop the spider back into his clutches. Unfortunately this was no ordinary clockwork spider. This was a *Harrods'* clockwork spider, and it would have given Lynford Christie a good run for his money. It sped across the department, bounced off a display of 'Caviar Crunchies' ('The Ultimate Feline Gastronomic Experience') and headed directly for the two unsuspecting, fur-coated, Chihuahua owners in the corner.

Probably if they'd seen it coming, it would have been all right. But their backs were turned and the first they knew of anything was when a *huge* black spider ran between them, closely followed by a despairing Mr Grovey who with one great lunge landed at their feet in a gasping heap.

The two ladies, unaccustomed to being assaulted by jet propelled spiders and lunatic teachers in Harrods' Pet Department (of all places!), screamed and fainted in perfect unison. The security guards arrived all of a bustle to find a pile of fur-clad ladies lying on top of a red-faced Mr Grovey who could be heard muttering, 'It's only clockwork.'

Meanwhile, Ms Shore and the rest of us in the group made a dignified exit from the room, pretending that the funny middle-aged hooligan in the corduroy jacket was nothing at all to do with us.

After Mr Grovey's performance in Harrods, the evening's entertainment – *Tales of the Unexpected* at the National Theatre – was a bit of an anticlimax. However, thinking about the day's events during the dark coach journey home, it seemed to me that the play's title summarised our day out nicely.

I bet if you'd asked Tony Peters, Mr Grovey and the two ladies in Harrods' Pet Department what they expected their day to hold, they would have thought that they knew. Tony would have said, 'No breakfast means no travel sickness', but he'd have been wrong. Mr Grovey would have said that the day's visits were all well arranged, but he'd have been wrong. The two ladies would have said that it was impossible to be assaulted by a middle-aged teacher and a clockwork spider in the Pet Department of Harrods, but they'd have been wrong! They, along with Mr Grovey and Tony, now had their own 'Tales of the Unexpected' to tell.

THINKY BIT

Thinking that you're right about something and actually *being* right about it can be two very different things. Sometimes it doesn't matter too much, because some things are matters of *opinion* and if you don't agree with your friends (or your teachers) then it doesn't really matter.

For example, you might think that Sega is better than Nintendo, whereas your friends might think that Nintendo is the best. That doesn't matter because in a way you can both be right. To you Sega really is best, yet to your friend Nintendo is tops. You're entitled to your opinion and they're entitled to theirs, and neither of you can be proved wrong!

But, say you thought that there were more games available for Sega than for Nintendo and your friend disagreed. Now only one of you can be right about this. It's not a matter of opinion, it's a matter of *fact* and if you were to look at a Sega catalogue and a Nintendo catalogue you would quickly be able to compare lists and see who was right.

Whether something is a matter of fact or opinion is important. Say you asked your friends the question, 'What is a Christian?' They might have their own ideas and opinions on the subject, but do they know the facts? One of them might think 'If you go to church every week you're a Christian'; someone else might say, 'Reading the Bible makes you a Christian'; another might suggest, 'A Christian is someone who doesn't eat lettuce'. They are entitled to their *opinions* but it is really important to understand that their opinions are not necessarily the *truth*. They can shout their opinions, argue about their opinions and laugh at you for not sharing their opinions, but none of these things make their opinions truth.

So, if you want to know what a Christian is, where do you go to find out? Although your friends and teachers may have their opinions, only God knows for sure, so it seems to make sense to go to his book, the Bible, to find the answer. What we find there may be a bit of a 'Tale of the Unexpected' to your friends, because it doesn't say that going to church makes you a Christian, nor that reading the Bible or praying makes you a Christian, and yes, you can be a Christian and eat lettuce! What does it say? Read on, it's really very simple.

Have you ever seen a shop that has been taken over by new owners? After they have swept it out, redecorated and restocked it, they will often put a sign in the window which says 'Under New Management'. This tells everyone that the old owners have gone and that the shop has started trading again. The outside of the shop may look the same but inside everything is new.

Becoming a Christian is just like that. Quite simply it's putting your life under new management, or appointing a new boss to be in charge of your life. When we try to run our own lives we frequently get in a mess. We make wrong choices, we hurt people (even people we care about) and we say, think and do things that later we are ashamed of. Why? Because if we are honest we must admit that we are not very good managers. Often we get it right, but sometimes we get it all wrong. In fact, the Bible says that 'everyone has sinned and is far away from God's saving presence' (Romans 3:23).

So a Christian is someone who has come to the point of *realising and admitting that they have made a mess of managing their life*. Christians are not 'goody goodies' who think they are always right, they are people who realise just how bad they can be and want to be better.

But Christians aren't just people who realise how many mistakes they have made. They are also people who have heard about Jesus and understand that he is the 'Mega Life-Manager'. The way he lived was incredible. He never made any mistakes, he always managed to put other people first, and he never had to apologise for saying or doing the wrong thing.

But Jesus is more than just the Mega Life-Manager. The Bible tells us that Jesus is the 'Cosmic King', 'far, far above any other king or ruler or dictator or leader' (Ephesians 1:21, *The Living Bible*). He is the 'Ultimate Mister Big', God's 'Captain Fantastic' and the Milky Way's 'Main Man'! What a person? Surely he's someone who we can trust with the management of our lives! !

A Christian is someone who is totally sold-out on wanting to be like Jesus, or to put it another way – a Christian is someone who recognises that there's *no one in the whole universe better at running a human life than Jesus*.

With these two important discoveries – (1) that they are a bad life-manager and have made countless mistakes, and (2) that Jesus is the Mega Life-Manager – a person who wants to become a Christian has to do two things.

Firstly, they must talk to God, admit that they have made mistakes by trying to run things their way, and ask to be forgiven for the wrong that they have done. At this point God promises to forgive them for every mistake and to no longer remember that they have ever done anything wrong! ! It's like he sweeps up all the mess that the old manager made, throws it in the dustbin and padlocks the lid.

The Bible says that God 'forgave all your sins, and blotted out the charges proved against you, the list of his commandments that you had not obeyed. He took this list of sins and destroyed it by nailing it to (Jesus') cross' (Colossians 2:13,14, *The Living Bible*). So a Christian is someone who need not feel guilty *whatever* has happened in the past.

Secondly, a person wanting to become a Christian must ask Jesus to be the new manager of their life, promising to live only for him from that point on. This is a big promise and should not be made lightly. At this point Jesus promises to come and live with you and to be your closest, bestest mate, helping you to *want* to do what he wants done and giving you the guts to do it.

The Bible puts it this way, when you ask Jesus to

become your new boss, God sets to 'work within you, helping you want to obey him, and then helping you do what he wants' (Philippians 2:13, *The Living Bible*).

So, a Christian is someone who is 'under new management' – their outside looks the same (they don't grow a second head! !) but inside everything is new because Jesus is now the new 'Manager'.

One final point. When a new manager is installed in a shop the staff obviously have to learn how to do what he wants. It's no good appointing a new manager only to find that half of the staff ignore him and carry on acting as though the old one was still in charge. That would lead to disaster and not much improvement in the service that the shop offered!

Similarly, when someone becomes a Christian and invites Jesus in as their new manager, they have to start doing what he says (which you discover by reading the Bible and listening to older Christians). It's no good calling yourself a Christian if *you* are still taking control of your life. This may mean that you have to change your attitude a bit, or start being kind to people that you have previously been rude to. It may mean spending your money to help other people instead of only on yourself. It may mean a whole lot of things, but when Mega Life-Manager Jesus takes over, we can be sure that *there will be changes*.

Jesus said, 'All who listen to my instructions and follow them are wise, like a man who builds his house on solid rock. . . But those who hear my instructions and ignore them are foolish, like a man who builds his house on sand. For when the rains and floods come, and storm winds beat against the house, it will fall with a mighty crash' (Matthew 7:24–27, *The Living Bible*).

A Christian is not just someone who listens to what

Jesus wants but *someone who is willing to do what Jesus wants even if it's difficult.*

SO WHAT?

1 Maybe some of the opinions you have heard at school about Christianity have confused you. You can now be more sure about the facts and feel more confident in what God says through the Bible.

2 If your friends are interested in knowing more about being a Christian, you could try to explain the key points from this chapter – or you could lend them this book (or get them their own copy!).

3 We've seen that a Christian is someone who listens to what Jesus wants and then does it. Check out how you are at discovering what Jesus wants and if you are being obedient to him by completing this checklist.

(a) I read my Bible regularly to discover more about Jesus.   Yes/No

(b) I pray each day to ask Jesus to help me manage my life.   Yes/No

(c) I go to church or a youth group to learn about following Jesus.   Yes/No

(d) When I'm at school I often try to think about how Jesus wants me to act.   Yes/No

(e) I can think of one example in the last week when I have deliberately chosen to do what Jesus wanted.   Yes/No

4 If you have got friends who think going to church or reading the Bible or praying make you a Christian, they aren't right, *but* they aren't completely wrong either! These three activities are vitally important but they are things that you do to grow stronger *once you have become a Christian*, not something that you do to make you a Christian in the first place.

To tell the truth

Once a term we have a Fire Practice. Actually this is a misleading name for it, since we don't practice *having* a fire, we practice what we should do in the event of a fire breaking out. Perhaps we should call it an 'If A Fire Really Happened This Is What We Would All Do' Practice. That would be more accurate, I think. Anyway for the purposes of this chapter, I'll stick to the more usual title because it's shorter (even though it's also wronger!).

The routine for a Fire Practice is that, once the bell starts ringing, everything should stop immediately and everyone in every class should silently file out of the room, leaving bags and coats behind, in order to assemble in tutor-group lines on the top tennis courts. The teacher in charge of each lesson should shut all windows and doors in the classroom before proceeding to the tennis courts. Whilst all this is happening, Mr Wilson, the Strict Deputy Head, collects the registers from the school office and takes them to the tennis courts where they are distributed to our form tutors, who then check that everyone in their group is out of the building.

Although they are vital to everyone's safety, Fire Practices always have a slightly unreal feel to them since everyone knows that there is no fire. You see, if you had a Fire Practice when no one was expecting it you could cause all sorts of problems in all sorts of lessons.

For example, just imagine if you were in a cookery lesson making a fruit cake. You have mixed all the ingredients together and just put the thing into the oven when 'Brring' – off goes the fire alarm. Now, do you leave the cake in the oven whilst you disappear to the tennis courts for 45 minutes or so – and risk starting a real fire – or do you turn the oven off and ruin the cake – and risk incurring your mum's anger? ('I didn't buy you all those ingredients for you to bring me home a mixed-fruit frisbee.')

Or imagine that you've just finished a cross-country run and you're having a shower when 'Brring' – off goes the you-know-what. Do you blushingly obey instructions and rush to the tennis courts without stopping for your possessions – which in this case includes all your clothes – or do you stop, dry and dress – and run the risk of being burned alive! You see the problem and the reason why Fire Practices are always announced before they happen.

However, one day the system was put to the test in a more realistic way. The full story didn't emerge until a bit later, so I'll try to put all the bits together. It was Mr Grovey, apparently, who took the phone call. A muffled voice said, 'There's a bomb somewhere in the school and if you don't evacuate the building you'll

Do you blushingly obey instructions and rush to the tennis courts. . . ?

be responsible for the consequences.'

Now, Mr Grovey had never been responsible for anything very much so he slammed the phone down and hot-footed it to Mrs Grillum, the headteacher, who was paid to be responsible for things like bomb scares. Mr Grovey reported what the voice had said and, after a few questions, Mrs Grillum rose from her chair and strode into the school office barking orders to anyone and everyone.

'Mrs Quince' – (school secretary) – 'ring the fire alarm immediately.'

'Mrs Maskell' – (Kind Deputy Head) – 'there's been a bomb warning and I think we should take it seriously. Phone the emergency services immediately.'

'You boy' – (Jason Smee, a trembling seventh year who'd only gone to the office to report a missing bus pass and who now found himself caught up in a suspected terrorist attack) – 'Run immediately and fetch Mr Wilson. Tell him that he should collect the registers and report to the tennis courts immediately!'

The excitement generated by an unannounced fire bell was considerably multiplied when word got around that this was a real live Bomb Scare. Of course the rumours got out of hand and pretty soon on the tennis courts, there were numerous accounts of what was going on. If you put all the stories together the overall picture that took shape would be a bit like this.

Mrs Grillum had been taken prisoner and, suspended by her toes from the school pool diving board, had been wired up to twenty pounds of Semtex explosive. The SAS, however, had already made plans for just such an emergency and were due to arrive by helicopter at any moment and with the use of stun grenades, would abseil down to rescue Mrs Grillum. Meanwhile an unknown terrorist organisation made up of disenchanted parents had targetted three short-range nuclear warheads on the school kitchens and were threatening to launch them if the price of school dinners wasn't reduced by 50%. As if this wasn't enough, anti-personnel mines had been laid on the school rugby pitch and the Bomb Squad had been called to sweep the whole area with mine detection equipment so that tonight's game against Westgate School 1st XV could be played.

And so it went on! After this build up the arrival of a fire engine and two policemen in a panda car was a bit of an anti-climax. The brave men of the local emergency services strolled through the school corridors prodding a few bags along the way and, after about an hour, announced that it was safe for us to re-enter the buildings and resume lessons.

Well, it all helped to break the boredom of school routine, but it also made me think how quickly and easily rumours can spread and how easily some people can be taken in. Camilla Miller, for example, spent the rest of the day with cotton wool in her ears in case the stun grenades, Semtex and the mines all went off at the same time as the missiles hit the kitchens!

THINKY BIT

Rumours spread and true stories quickly get exaggerated as new bits are added on at each retelling. Maybe some of your school friends think that the Bible stories about Jesus are a bit like that. They may think that there was a real person called Jesus who lived in Israel nearly two thousand years ago. He was probably quite a well-known person, maybe a clever teacher, and he had a pretty big fan club. When he died (so the story goes) his fan club started making up stories about him, exaggerating the things he did, so that he looked even more impressive than he really was, and also so that the fan club (called 'the Church') would continue to get more members. Some of them even spread the tale that they had seen him alive again after he was buried! The Superglue Sandwich question here would go something like, 'But how do you know that the Bible is true? Hasn't it all just been made up?'.

Is that the truth? Can we believe what the Bible says about Jesus? What about the incredible miracles that we read about? Are they true? If not, how do we know anything about him at all? Here are seven reasons why you can trust what the Bible tells you about Jesus:

1 The people who wrote Jesus' life story actually knew, him! If you were asking someone to write your life story, you would obviously want it to be someone who knew you well. Is that the case for the books in the Bible which tell us about Jesus?

Let's take John as an example. He wrote a book about Jesus and he wasn't someone who had only a vague idea about who Jesus was – he was one of his best friends. Matthew, another of Jesus' best friends, wrote a book about Jesus' life, too. Matthew and John didn't arrive on the scene ten years or so after Jesus had died! No, they actually *lived* with him for about three years. So surely they would be able to write the truth about him.

2 It'll come as no surprise to you to know that the things Jesus did were never filmed for TV and his words were never recorded for radio. So how did people remember what he said and did? Well, they memorised it!

At this point I can hear your little grey cells clinking together as you think, Oh yeah likely story. I'm sure *I* could never remember everything my best friend said and did for the last three years. No, you probably couldn't, but firstly the Bible doesn't tell us *everything* that Jesus said and did – only certain important and outstanding bits. I'm pretty sure that you would have remembered if your best friend had walked across the school swimming pool or made two sardine sandwiches and five bags of crisps feed the whole school one lunch time!

Secondly, in Jesus' time, because they didn't have cassettes, videos and the like, they were far more used to remembering huge chunks of stuff than we are.

Many Jewish men would be able to recite most of the first five books of the Bible off by heart! School teaching was done by memory – no exercise books, A4 file paper or computer disks. All this means that it's not so difficult to believe that the information recorded about Jesus in our Bibles was remembered, and eventually written down, accurately.

3 One of the ways in which people decide whether an ancient book is telling the truth or not is by finding out how many years passed between the events that the book describes and the date that the book was written.

Say a Roman slave – let's call him Venomous Mucus – performed the first ever rap. If one week later his friend, Nauseous Linctus, wrote it down we'd probably trust him to write it fairly accurately. If, however, Nauseous left it two weeks before he wrote it down we might be a bit less certain that what he wrote was what Venomous had performed. And if Nauseous was really lazy and took the next twenty years off before scribing the rap, we might take some convincing that what he wrote bore any resemblance to what was first sung.

However, to a historian twenty years is nothing, and some famous ancient history books were written a hundred years or more after the events they describe. What about the Bible? Well, some of the books in the New Testament were written not hundreds of years but no more than thirty-five after Jesus died! This short gap between his life and the first books being written about him is a further piece of evidence for the truthfulness of the Bible.

4 One of the important things to follow from the last point is that, if the books about Jesus were written quite

soon after his life, then there would still be people alive who actually knew him when the books were being circulated. If Matthew's book was full of made-up stories, there would have been people around when it was first read who would have remembered the truth about Jesus. They would have had Matthew's book destroyed as a hoax. The fact that the books by Matthew, Mark, Luke and John were all accepted as true by those who knew Jesus and remembered the things he had done and said, helps us to know that we too can believe them. Incidentally, we should remember that many of the first Christians were killed for their faith. If they thought the stories about Jesus were just made up by a first century Roald Dahl, they surely wouldn't have been prepared to be murdered for what they believed.

5 If the events of Jesus' life described in the Bible had happened on Mars, we would have difficulty picturing them or double-checking their truth, since day trips to Mars are expensive and not many people go there. (Well, actually, no one goes there!) However, the Bible tells us that Jesus lived on our planet in the country of Israel, so to help us check out the stories we could go to Israel and try to dig up the past to find out if the places and people that Jesus knew really existed. Many people have been doing just that for many, many years and, the more they have dug up, the more they have found to show that the Bible stories about Jesus are true.

For example, in John's book about Jesus he says that 'near the Sheep Gate in Jerusalem there is a pool with five porches' (John 5:2). For centuries no one could find any evidence that such a pool existed. But in the 1930s a French archaeologist called Pere Vincent was able to find the remains of just such a pool, surrounded by five porches.

Another example. Luke writes about a man called Gallio who he says is the Roman governor (or proconsul) of a place called Achaia in Greece. A man called Tacitus wrote a history book at about the same time that Luke wrote his book and he mentions Gallio as well, but he doesn't say that he was a Roman governor. For centuries 'experts' believed Tacitus (who wasn't a Christian) and disbelieved Luke. But recently an inscription has been found which confirms Luke's account that Gallio really was the Roman governor of Achaia.

Neither of these examples are earth-shattering, but they do add weight to the Bible's account of the life and times of Jesus.

6 Perhaps your friends might say something like this: 'If this Jesus bloke was so great, how come you only read about him in the Bible? How come no one else mentions him in their books?' Well, the truth is – they do! ! Matthew, Mark, Luke and John wrote loads about Jesus because they set out to write his life story, but there were other people at the time writing books and letters and official documents. Although these people weren't writing mainly about the life of Jesus, they couldn't ignore the fact that such an incredible person was around. So Jesus gets a mention in several of their books, too.

We've already mentioned Tacitus. In one of his books he writes about the Roman emperor Nero blaming Christians for causing the great fire that destroyed Rome. He then adds:

Christus (Christ) from whom their name is derived was executed at the hands of the procurator Pontius Pilate in the reign of Tiberius.

This brief reference to Jesus' death fits in well with the details recorded in the Bible. Josephus, a Jewish historian, wrote this:

At this time there was a wise man who was called Jesus. And his conduct was good, and he was known to be virtuous. And many people from among the Jews and the other nations became his disciples. Pilate condemned him to be crucified and to die. . .

So here again, in the books of other writers we can see evidence for the truth of the Bible.

7 Finally, it's also worth thinking about the fact that the life of Jesus has had such a huge impact on the earth. Our calendar measures the number of years since his birth (2000 AD stands for 2000 Anno Domini, which means 'the 2000th Year of our Lord'). The Bible is the world's best-selling book, translated into more languages than any other. The Church is a huge worldwide family of people who still try to follow Jesus. Sunday – the day Jesus came back to life – is recognised as a special day in many countries of the world. And so on. If Jesus never existed, or if he was just a first century nutcase, then surely history would have forgotten all about him.

In the book of Acts the religious leaders were getting jealous of the popularity of Jesus' followers, so they had them arrested and commanded them to stop talking about Jesus. Peter and the others refused and said that they *must* keep talking about Jesus because that's what he'd told them to do. At this point, when everyone was getting pretty angry, Gamaliel, one of the members of the council stood up, told everyone to cool it and said:

> Leave them alone! If what they have planned and done is of human origin, it will disappear, but if it comes from God, you cannot possibly defeat them. You could find yourselves fighting against God (Acts 5:38,39).

Gamaliel was right. The facts are that what the apostles were talking about hasn't disappeared – even after nearly two thousand years – because it wasn't just make-believe but really was 'from God'.

SO WHAT?

1 When your friends start to talk about the Bible as though it were a book of fairy stories, you can now talk to them about some of the evidence for taking it more seriously than that! Which piece of evidence did you find most convincing? Re-read that section so you can explain it to your friends.

2 When you read the Bible you can do so trusting that what you are reading really is true.

3 Because the Bible is true it's important to read it carefully and allow what we read to sink in. Racing through the Bible like we might race through the *Beano* or the *TV Times* is hardly likely to help us understand it.

Many people find it helpful to read the Bible with the help of some notes which explain what the Bible is

45

saying. Scripture Union produces notes for different age ranges. You'll probably find a selection at your nearest Christian bookshop. Alternatively, if you write to them at this address they will send you some advice about the notes that might be best for you – Scripture Union, 130 City Road, London EC1V 2NJ.

4 Because the Bible is true, it would be wrong to try and twist it to make it say something different. For example, I might like to believe that I can be rude to my parents, but the Bible clearly says that we should 'respect' our parents (Exodus 20:12)! That's plain enough and so my only choice is whether to obey it or not. If what the Bible says is true, I can't try to make it say something it doesn't so that I can do what I want! !

The incredible exploits of nothing

The pattern of life at our school is very predictable. It's regulated by our timetable, which tells us where we must be, when we must be there and more or less what we will do once we have arrived. For ten months from September to July we go through the same series of lessons over and over again. It was hardly surprising, then, that towards the end of last summer term, when we were given our new timetable for this school year, there was a sense of excitement in the air.

I suppose everyone had their idea of what they wanted on their new timetable. Some wanted Miss Slipman for Maths because she had a reputation for being soft ... er ... easy to get on with, but others wanted Mr Barnes because he never set much homework. Some wanted Science *after* lunch because the labs were next to the dining hall so we could drop our bags there on the way in to eat and leave them there through lunch time. But others wanted Science *before* lunch because the prospect of cutting up sheeps' eyes on a full stomach was too horrible to even think about.

As for me, my strongest wish was for Games on Friday afternoon. Friday afternoon was the worst time of the week to concentrate on books, experiments, tests and the like, so it seemed to me that it was the best time to get out and run around letting off steam.

Mrs Bellingham was our tutor, so she was the one to announce to us our new timetable. She dictated, we wrote.

'Monday, period 1, Maths in A12 with Mr Barnes...' (Groans.)

'Period 2, Drama in G16 with Mr Grovey...' (Murmurs of, 'Could be worse'.)

'Period 3, Languages in A9 with Mademoiselle Lafitte, the new French assistant...' (One or two whistles, quickly silenced by one of Mrs Bellingham's hard stares.)

'Period 4, Design and Technology in T6 with Mr Stanley...' (Whispers of 'Oh no, not The Knife'.)

'Tuesday, period 1, Games.'

What? ! Oh cosmic catastroscope! Not on a Tuesday morning, or any morning – please! If Friday afternoons were the best time for Games, any morning was the worst. It meant getting hot and smelly early in the day and staying that way all afternoon; it meant having to carry festering, muddy kit around in your school bag for hours on end.

But it was no good. Tuesday morning Games were announced and all this year Tuesday morning Games it has been. Until now it hadn't been too bad, I suppose, but now was mid-May, the time of year when the school's swimming programme started. Very nice I'm sure for those schools with access to indoor heated pools, but ours was outdoors and very much unheated!

Our pool was outdoors and very much unheated!

Mid-May might pretend to be 'early summer', but first thing on a mid-May Tuesday morning, when you're standing shivering next to an unheated swimming pool wearing nothing but your cozzie, you're certain that mid-May, far from 'early summer' should still be recognised as 'late winter'.

This particular morning, having broken the ice on the pool, those of us who could already swim had to practise our diving. This involved dropping a bright yellow brick into the deep end and then taking it in turns to dive to retrieve it. Meanwhile Mr Gray, our Games teacher, helped the non-swimmers in the shallow end.

All went well at the deep end until Mike Rogers, having dived to retrieve the brick, decided to put it back in the water by shot-putting it up the pool rather than by gently lowering it in as we'd been instructed. He stood on the edge of the pool and gave the brick a mighty heave into what he imagined to be an area of unoccupied water. Unfortunately, at precisely the time and place that Mike's brick entered the water, Steve Fox's head popped up as he emerged gasping for breath from his attempt to swim the length of the pool under water.

The brick only caught him a glancing blow, but it caused a nasty gash on the side of his head all the same. Fortunately there were no sharks or piranhas in the pool or Steve's bleeding wound might have attracted some very unwelcome attention! As it was, it soon attracted the attention of Mr Gray, who dressed it with such a long bandage that it made Steve's head look sort of mummified.

Mr Gray then turned on the possible culprits.

'OK, so who threw the brick?'

Silence. Apparently, Mike wasn't about to own up, and we weren't about to confess on his behalf.

'Who threw the brick?' More menacing this time but still no response.

'For the last time, who threw the brick?' Silence, then, 'No one, Sir.'

Mike had spoken up – but not with the answer that anyone expected!

'No one?! What do you mean "no one", you stupid boy?'

'No one threw the brick, Sir. We were all swimming about, and then we saw the brick sail overhead and land on Steve's head, Sir. I saw something like it in a

James Bond film once. Perhaps it was a remote-controlled brick, Sir, or. . .'

'Silence! ! What are you talking about? Remote controlled brick! ! What do you take me for?'

Fortunately, Mike chose not to answer that question! ! However, he had said a bit more than he should and, with that uncanny knack which most teachers have, Mr Gray identified Mike as the guilty party.

Afterwards I started to wonder why Mike had given such a strange answer. Panic, I suppose. The idea that a brick could just pick itself up and fly down the pool was clearly idiotic. If the thing was going to move, someone had to move it. Didn't they?

THINKY BIT

Many people believe that the whole, enormous universe, the beautiful world that we live in, all life and . . . well, everything just 'happened' to come into being entirely on its own. There are lots of theories about how this might have come about, but the idea that Nothing can develop into a vast complicated Something with absolutely No One in charge of proceedings is like believing the brick in the story could have just flown across the pool on its own. The just 'happened' story of the world goes a bit like this:

THE INCREDIBLE EXPLOITS OF NOTHING

In the beginning there was Nothing. No world, no universe, no Ronald MacDonald, no humans and no Sumo wrestlers. Absolutely Nothing.

After several million years Nothing got bored and decided to become Something. And it wasn't long before Something got lonely and decided to split into two. (Just by chance he found he had the ability to do this.) Each of Something's two halves joined the trend and they divided. There were then six Somethings.

Eventually there were so many Somethings that they decided to join together into groups and form into galaxies of planets. Just by chance they all found that they could float around without bumping into each other too much.

Just by chance on one little planet – called 'Earth' because most of its surface was covered by water (!) – there were lots of terrible thunder storms and, just by chance one day, in a particularly vicious one, a bolt of lightning hit a muddy puddle, which just happened to have the right chemicals in it to make Life.

The heat of the lightning caused these chemicals to join together and, just by chance, the first little Living Something had been created.

Living Something like his Grandad, Nothing, got bored and lonely, and decided to grow up. After a long time Living Something just by chance found that he had grown up into a fish.

Living Something Fish would occasionally look out on all the air and land, and get quite dissatisfied with his watery living conditions.

Eventually one particular Living Something Fish made a decision which was to affect the whole of the rest of history – he decided to grow wings and become a bird.

Fortunately for Living Something Bird he found there was just enough oxygen for him to breathe and enough things for him to eat (all just by chance, of course).

Zillions more years passed by and, just by chance, birds became animals, and animals eventually summoned up all their energy and put together all their best ideas and became Human Being Somethings.

Human Being Somethings looked at the world and the universe and said how clever it was of Nothing to become Something and wasn't it incredible that, just by chance, the world was such a beautiful place.

Human Being Somethings just by chance got really clever – far more clever than any of their ancestors – and they found out a lot about the world they lived in. They found out that the earth was round and spinning, yet no one had ever fallen off. They discovered that if conditions on earth were just a little different – a bit more oxygen, a little less gravity, half as much forest or a bit more ocean – it would be impossible for Human Being Somethings to live on Earth at all!

Humans looked at all this incredible evidence about their world and saw what a complicated place it was. They began to see how well-made it was and how each part seemed to have its own job to do. They saw all that Nothing had made and they said it was very good.

One or two humans began to ask sticky questions like, 'If our world is so wonderful – almost like it has been cleverly put together – wouldn't it be more sensible to assume that it started with a Someone, an Incredible Inventor, who planned things to be like this, rather than believing in hundreds of miracles making everything just happen by lucky chance?' But everyone laughed at the idea that there was a Someone involved in making the earth so beautiful and complicated. Instead they went on trying to discover how No One had got hold of Nothing and made Everything.

Of course not everyone believes in Nothing being quite so intelligent and powerful! Millions of Christians, for example, find that the Bible's account of an intelligent God making our well-designed world makes far more sense of the facts. This point is well demonstrated by a story told about the famous scientist, Sir Isaac Newton.

Sir Isaac Newton was a Christian. He discovered a lot about the way the earth works. In his study he had a big model of the planets in their different orbits. It was very impressive. One day another scientist (who did not believe in God) came to visit Sir Isaac for the first time and asked him who had made the model for him because he would like one the same. Sir Isaac said, 'No one made it!' His friend looked at him as though he was mad and repeated the question.

'Who made the model of the universe?'

'No one!'

'You're trying to tell me that this complicated working model just appeared in your study with no help from anyone at all?'

Sir Isaac said, 'Well, you tell me that the entire universe just happened all by itself with no help from anyone. So surely you can believe that this little model could have just happened.'

Of course his friend had no answer. However, the Bible does have an answer for how such a complicated and beautiful world came to exist. The Bible says that there was Someone involved in making the world. It's not all just one enormous lucky chance, but instead has been planned by the greatest, most powerful Someone imaginable – God. This is what the Bible says:

> The world and all that is in it belong to the
>   Lord;
> The earth and all who live on it are his.
> He built it . . .
>
> (Psalm 24)

> When I look at the sky, which you have made,
> at the moon and the stars, which you set in their
> places –
> what is man, that you think of him; mere man,
> that you care for him?
> Yet you made him inferior only to yourself . . .
>
> (Psalm 8)

> God looked at everything he had made,
>   and he was very pleased.
>
> (Genesis 1:31)

The Bible doesn't tell us very much at all about *how* God made the world. If God tried to tell us exactly how he did it, our brains wouldn't be able to cope with the overload! But, bit by bit, science may be discovering things about the way God worked when he made everything. However, the point that the Bible makes is very clear – there was Someone at work in the creation of the world – a great, intelligent, powerful God.

SO WHAT?

1 Because we live in God's world, we should listen to what he says about how to live in it. For best results, follow the Maker's instructions.

2 Because we live in God's world, we should look after it for him and not treat it as though we owned it. We're only 'borrowing' it from God, and we must always remember that one day he'll want to know how well we've been looking after his property.

3 Because we can see how fantastic the world and everything in it is, it helps us to praise God and understand him better. A fantastic world must have had a fantastic Maker! !

4 When our friends say they don't believe in God, we can remember that the very world we live in is evidence for God's existence. The Bible says, 'Since earliest times men have seen the earth and sky and all God made, and have known of his existence and great eternal power' (Romans 1:20, *The Living Bible*).

Monkey business

Break time had gone well. We'd been let out of English as soon as the bell had rung and I'd made a dash for the school tuck shop. Being at the front of the queue meant that you could ensure your day's ration of Pepsi and Mars Bars. Straight after that I'd found a quiet corner to eat the remainder of my packed lunch (most of it had been consumed during registration), and then Tony Peters invited me to join in an experiment that he and some of his mates were about to perform. The basic idea was to attempt to break the world record for cramming people into music practice rooms.

This attempt to enter *The Guinness Book of Records* could only be attempted on Thursday break times, because on Thursdays Mr Grant – the Art teacher – who is supposed to be on duty patrolling the stretch of corridor next to the music practice rooms, actually spends most of his break rolling his own cigarettes in the large store cupboard in the art room (where he hopes the Head won't notice that he's skiving).

Anyway, while he rolled his own suicide sticks, Tony Peters aimed to enter the record books. The previous record was thirty-four people, but Tony Peters reckoned we could nearly double that by cramming the room with older kids who had small kids on their shoulders.

We duly lined up outside Music Room 1. Tony arranged us in pairs – one large, one small. On the word of command, the smaller of each pair climbed onto the shoulders of their larger partner and the line of piggy-backed record-breakers slowly began to file into Music Room 1. All was going well, and we had managed to get thirty standing (a total of sixty people), when trouble struck. Florence Torrance (with Xanthe Smith on her shoulders) decided to increase the room's capacity still further by clambering on top of the piano, thus creating more floor space. Florence was noted for her brain power but not for her agility, and she was half way through the manoeuvre when she and Xanthe parted company.

It was probably just as well for Xanthe that there were, by then, fifty-nine other people in the room, or she would have hit the floor with quite a crash. As it was, she hit Darren Smith with quite a crash, who hit James Kirkby *and* Fiona Campbell with quite another crash. In fact, such a lot of crashing went on in such a short amount of time that afterwards it was impossible to tell who had hit who. The only thing that was certain was that somewhere in all the confusion Stuart Hooper's nose got crashed and started to bleed. Unfortunately Stuart was on the shoulders of the tallest person in the room and most of the rest of us got generously showered.

It's amazing how much blood the human being keeps up its nose! Just to look at an average nose you would maybe guess that it contained about an egg cup full, but judging from the evidence of sixty school-uniform white shirts, now with the very latest in designer blood spots, you could only conclude that Stuart Hooper's nasal passages were a lot bigger inside than out! As we evacuated Music Room 1, observers said we looked like the after effects of an explosion in a tomato soup factory.

Sadly one of those observers was Mr Wilson, the Strict Deputy Head. Now you might think that anyone would be *pleased* to be at the scene of the setting of a new world record, but not Mr Wilson! No, he did not appear at all impressed as he watched sixty blood-stained people evacuate Music Room 1.

'What's going on here?' he began after a brief inspection revealed that the room was now empty of would-be record-breakers. 'I don't know what you think you're doing, but if you think that it's at all funny or clever to behave like a load of animals, then I suggest you learn to think differently very quickly.' The lecture went on in similar vein for several minutes, but I switched off at that point because Mr Wilson's last comment had made me think.

Was it fair to say that in attempting to scale new heights of human achievement by breaking the world record for the number of people in a music practice room we were behaving like 'a load of animals'? Which animals did this sort of thing? I began to wonder. In my mind I tried to visualise an animal equivalent.

Maybe at night all the cats in our neighbourhood get together under cover of darkness to see how many of them can cram into the phone box on the corner of our street. Or perhaps all the slugs in the garden try to squeeze into one fallen apple. No, silly idea. But maybe

I tried to visualise an animal equivalent.

other countries have animal record-breakers. Is there, for example, a world record High Jump for Giraffes, or a Hippopotamus Synchronised Swimming Champion, or an annual Most-Monkeys-Up-A-Tree Award? Or then again. . .

I was brought back to reality with a bump as I heard the end of Mr Wilson's reproving lecture, '. . . and seeing as how you all like staying inside during break so much, I'll see you all in room G10 for every break time this week.'

THINKY BIT
You may have come across the idea that human beings (that's you and me) are sort of top-of-the-range mem-

bers of the animal family. (It's highly likely that some of your teachers and friends at school believe this.) In other words, they believe that a long time ago, their great-great-great-great-great-great-great-great-(etc!) grandparents were not human beings but apes. More than that, they believe that the great-great-great-great-great-(etc!) grandparents of these apes were not apes but fish! There are lots of difficulties in believing that apes came from fish and that we came from apes. But one of the biggest difficulties is not the fact that we *look* different but that *inside* we *are* very different.

Animals may be like us in some ways, for example they breathe the same air, many have similar bodies with lungs, eyes, heart and nose, etc., and they eat, sleep and eventually die. We even talk about animals having a 'personality' all of their own, which means that no two dogs or cats appear to be exactly the same. But, for all the similarities, there are some huge and obvious differences between animals and humans.

How can we explain the fact that there is this difference between us and animals? Well, the Bible has an answer and it's a pretty good one (surprise, surprise!).

The first chapter of the Bible holds the clue to the puzzle. In Genesis chapter one we learn that the world is not a gigantic accident but was made by God. As God saw each different part of what he had made, he said that it was good – he liked it and was well pleased with it.

He appreciated the beauty in what he had made and thought that it was so beautiful it was a shame to keep it all to himself. So, when everything else had been formed, God the Father had a chat with Jesus and the Holy Spirit (who, according to the Bible were *all* involved in creating the world), and they decided to

61

make one more thing – a human being. But when they made the first human, they decided to use a special ingredient completely missing from all the rest of the things they had made. Let's listen in to their discussion:

> And now we will make human beings; they will be like us and resemble us. (Genesis 1:26)

And this is exactly what they did!

> So God created human beings, making them to be like himself. He created them male and female... (Genesis 1:27)

Wow!! The incredible decision they made as they talked together was that when God made the first humans he would make them in some way *like himself!* The special ingredient in people that is missing from the rest of the animal world, and which explains the differences between us, is nothing less than 'God-likeness'.

This doesn't mean that we *are* gods, nor does it mean we *look* like God. It does mean that, unlike any animal, we're made to be like God inside. This makes us different to the animal world in many ways. Here are some of them:

1 Creativity – if you put a pile of Lego in front of a small child, it won't be long before he or she begins to try and make something out of the pieces. The many great inventions that humans have made all point to our fantastic ability to create, whether it's cars, buildings, computers or aeroplanes. This ability, far beyond anything seen in the animal world, comes from God,

the Great Creator, putting his likeness in us.

2 Intelligence – you may find it hard to believe by looking at your school report, but humans are owners of extraordinary brain power! However intelligent my dog is when she obeys commands like 'Sit', or 'Roll over', she is never going to be the next Einstein! The gap between any animal's intelligence and ours is so great because we're made *in the likeness of* the 'Ultimate Intelligence' – God – and they're simply made *by* God.

3 Right and wrong – all human beings seem to have an inbuilt sense of 'right and wrong'. Even a very small child will say things like, 'That's not fair, she's got more sweets than me!' But how does the child know what 'fair' is? Where does the idea that some things are right and some things are wrong come from?

Part of it comes from our parents and teachers, who teach us about right and wrong. But there also seems to be a sort of 'built-in understanding' that some things are good and some things bad, some things 'fair' and some things 'unfair'. We all have a 'conscience' which starts to trouble us and make us feel guilty when we do something that goes against our sense of what is right. If humans are just animals, it seems odd that we have these strong feelings of right and wrong when other animals do not. On the other hand, if we're not just 'animals', but special parts of God's creation made like him, then immediately we can understand that God's sense of 'right and wrong' has been given to us. This will inevitably make us different from the animal world.

4 Nice and nasty – human beings seem to have a clear

idea of what is nice and what is naff, what is beautiful and what is ugly. People's ideas of what is beautiful have led to some great creative achievements in music, drama, art or sport. We all have our own ideas of what's beautiful, but when was the last time you saw a monkey admiring a great work of art, or a rat enjoying a great piece of music?

Do you remember when God made the world, as each new stage of his plan was completed, he took a step back, looked at the sights, listened to the sounds, sniffed the smells and said, 'That's good'? It's no wonder is it that we humans, being made like God, do exactly the same when we see, hear or smell something beautiful.

So are we humans just grown up monkeys – a more advanced form of life than our great-great-great-great-great-great-great-great-great- (etc!) grandparents? No! A closer look at who we are and how we live shows that there are just too many differences between us and other animals to believe the 'grown-up monkey' theory. We've also seen that the Bible gives us good answers for *why* we are so different.

SO WHAT?
1 Since human beings are created with God's blueprint, there's no such thing as a worthless human being. *All* human beings are to be respected, and it's wrong to look down on someone just because they are male or female, because they have a different colour skin, or because they just don't 'fit in'.

One of the most common ways of putting people down is by telling unkind jokes about them. Jokes can be funny, but they can also be cruel and unkind, so be careful when you tell jokes that you're not mocking people, all of whom are special to God. You should say sorry to God if you have ever put down another person by being rude to them – to their face or behind their back – by telling jokes about them or by ignoring them.

2 We should thank God for the fantastic privilege of being made like him. Our intelligence, our ability to have fun making things, the pleasure we get from music, books or sport, our close friendships and our ability to choose to do what's good and right, all make life enjoyable and a far cry from the sort of existence known to any animal.

3 When your friends (or teachers) say that humans came from monkeys you can remember that, however many similarities there are, there are lots more differences. Even if you can't explain them all, you can feel confident in knowing that there are good reasons for believing that humans are special – not just top-of-the-range monkeys! !

4 One of the dangers in telling people that they're just 'grown-up monkeys' is that they start to behave as if they are! What do I mean?

Well, animals do what they want, when they want. They have no great sense of right and wrong. So if, for example, my dog's hungry and she sees the cat's food lying around uneaten, she'll gobble it down. If the cat then comes along and finds her food's been nicked, and spots Geraldine the gerbil having a walkabout, she'll more than likely satisfy her hunger pangs at Geraldine's expense!

The dog won't think, 'No, it's very wrong of me to

steal someone else's food, so I won't do it'. And the cat won't think, 'Murder is wrong. However hungry I am, I'll wait until I'm next fed'!!

It's not very kind or right to steal or murder, but this is how animals operate. Sadly, as we know from the newspapers and TV news, this is also how many people behave – taking what's not theirs, even killing to steal someone else's property. There have always been people prepared to do these things, but it seems that there's an increasing trend. Perhaps it's not surprising when people brought up to believe that they're animals start to act as if they are!

You know you're not an animal. *You* know what's right and wrong, and *you* know that *you* have the power to choose what's right and refuse to do what's wrong. Don't act like an animal – act as God intended.

Mem'n'Trem the Thunder Men

Our school's Music Department is run by Mrs Glen. She's OK – for a teacher. On top of teaching classes all day, she runs a choir, a brass band, a steel band and an orchestra in the lunch hours. Towards the end of each term all of these groups perform in the School Concert which is held in the main school hall.

One of the good things about Mrs Glen is that she likes to encourage a wide range of musical styles to flourish in the school. This term, for example, the choir had been rehearsing versions of pop songs, the brass band had been blaring out an arrangement called 'Bach's Best Bits for Brass', and the steel band's version of 'My Old Man's A Dustbin' was sure to bring the house down at the concert!

It was two weeks before the concert and rehearsals were going well. Mrs Glen was on the point of making her final decision about the content of the programme, when, during break time, she had a visit from Jon Membury and Graham Trembel who asked whether they would be allowed to perform in the show. Their request took Mrs Glen by surprise since Jon and Graham were more famous for their artistic ability (they once covered the bike sheds with spray-on graffiti) than for their musical accomplishments. Upon further inquiry, however, they claimed to be the sole members of a rock band called 'Mem'n'Trem the Thunder Men'. Jon played drums and Graham (apparently) was a finger-lickingly slick guitarist.

Mrs Glen was uncertain what to do. On the one hand she did need a few extra items to fill out the concert programme and she did want the range of music played to be as wide as possible. On the other hand, she'd never heard 'Mem'n'Trem the Thunder Men' play, and something deep inside her told her that she should be cautious.

Unfortunately there was no time for Mrs Glen to have a preview of their music since the programme for the concert was due at the printers that very day. So, against her better judgement, she included Jon and Graham on the programme between the orchestra's rendition of 'Guns'n'Roses For Easy Strings', and the choir's vegetarian show-stopper 'Sheep May Safely Graze'.

John and Graham were extremely grateful and promised to practise regularly for their part in the show. They told Mrs Glen that they would like to play a selection of Elvis Presley songs which they had entitled 'Heartbreak at Blue Hound Dog Rock'. During the following two weeks Mrs Glen had to trust herself to Mem and Trem's reports on how practise sessions were going because they were unable to transport their gear into school to give her a live demonstration. According to them, however, all was going well.

Eventually the great day dawned and the hall was prepared for the concert. Graham's dad delivered an ominously large amplification system to the school and Jon's mum brought what at first sight looked like a car load of hatboxes but, on closer inspection, proved to be Jon's drum kit in its variously-sized carrying cases. The gear was carried to the school hall by willing friends, and Jon and Graham spent the afternoon break putting it all together.

It was 7.50 pm and the concert had started well. The brass band, which had brasso'd itself to a state of highly polished visual excellence, had got things going with a foot-tappingly lively account of 'When The Saints'. The orchestra had pluckily scraped its way through its 'Guns'n'Roses' arrangement. The moment arrived for the curtains to be drawn back on 'Mem'n'Trem the Thunder Men'. Mrs Glen thought she was prepared for anything, but the sight which greeted the audience as the curtains were wound back was, to put it mildly, unexpected.

Jon Membury was seated at his drum kit. He was wearing a black T-shirt, across which, in large, pink, fluorescent letters, was the legend 'I Hit Heads (And Deputies)'. Around his head was a tartan scarf, tied in the best Apache style, and his two earrings, each with skull-and-cross-bones emblem, glittered menacingly in the spot lights' beams. Graham Trembel, meanwhile, stood centre stage, his jeans slashed at the knee and the collar on his leather-look jacket firmly fixed in the 'up' position. Around his waist was a 10 cm deep leather belt decorated with what seemed like hundreds of small metal studs. The total effect was topped off with a fake 'tattoo' of a spider crawling across his left cheek.

If, at that point the curtains had been drawn back across the stage, no one could have argued that they had just witnessed *the* most notable event of the whole evening. However, as Mrs Glen was wondering whether to order just such an action, her indecision was interrupted by the first major earthquake ever to hit Great Britain. At least that's what she and all the school Governors sitting in the front row assumed had happened, based on the evidence of a strongly vibrating floor, dust and debris being dislodged from the beams high up in the hall roof, and an ear-achingly loud rumbling noise.

In actual fact, all that had occurred was the commencement of 'Heartbreak at Blue Hound Dog Rock'. No one actually had blood running from their ears, but it must have been merely a decibel away from bursting forth.

Even at that point, when it seemed that no more damage could be inflicted by the Thunder Men, things took a final turn for the worse. 'Mem'n'Trem's' debut had been allotted a three minute slot in the programme and in fairness they did aim to finish on time. But 'Trem', slightly stagestruck by his first public performance, got lost (musically speaking) and resorted to repeating the same eight-bar riff over and over again until he could remember how to continue. Sadly for Mrs Glen's reputation, the Governing Body's eardrums and the school hall's roof, it took him a long time to remember, and this lengthened the allocated three minutes into a seemingly eternal seven.

When they had finished there was an awe-struck silence in the hall. This was eventually broken by wild cheering from the members of the brass band, steel band and choir, which was slowly joined by polite –

No one actually had blood running from their ears but it was merely a decibel away. . .

it muted – applause from the rest of the half-dazed audience.

In the interval Mem and Trem, seemingly unaware of the stir that they had just caused, eagerly sought out Mrs Glen.

'Well, Miss, what did you think? Not bad, eh?' said Mem, rashly fishing for a compliment.

'Yeah, sorry about getting lost and all that, but we won't charge anything extra for them other four minutes,' joked Trem, unwisely bright.

'We got a good load of cheering at the end though, Miss, so can't have been too much of a dive, eh?'

'After that I suppose you'll want us to star in all

of your end-of-term dos. How about the School Carol Service? We do a good Christmas number called "A Rave in the Manger, Start Banging Your Head".'

Mrs Glen, looking a little grey I thought, turned away without a word and set about trying to salvage the rest of the evening by preparing everyone for the second half of the programme.

THINKY BIT

Mem and Trem couldn't understand the problem. What was wrong with their music? Mrs Glen couldn't understand how Mem and Trem couldn't see that *everything* was wrong with their music! ! Two completely opposite views over one piece of music. Do you ever have clashes of opinion like that with your parents over a piece of music, or a TV programme or film that you want to watch? Most of us do at some time, and if we've been prevented from watching a film on TV that all our friends have seen, we can feel a bit left out – or even a lot left out! And if they ask us *why* we didn't watch or listen in, we can get that old Superglue Sandwich feeling and not really know how to answer.

So let's think for a bit about how to decide what to watch on TV and what music to listen to. As always, we'll turn to the Bible for a bit of advice.

1 'Don't copy the behaviour and customs of this world, but be a new and different person with a fresh newness in all you do and think.' This verse, from Romans 12:2 (*The Living Bible*), is a good starting point for deciding what to watch and listen to. We belong to God – we're under new management (see page 29) – so just because someone else watches a particular TV programme or listens to a particular group, that doesn't mean we all

have to copy their 'behaviour and customs'.

Sadly many people, old and young, never stop to think about what they watch and listen to, but just assume that if everyone else does it, it must be OK. But God encourages us to be fresh thinkers, to be willing to be different in all that we do and think. Are you ready for the challenge or are you determined to go with the flow of your friends, even if the flow goes down the drain into the sewer?!

2 Jesus' friends had some very clear (and very wrong) ideas about what made them right with God. For example, they believed that if you ate the wrong sorts of food you would be 'unclean' and God would not want anything to do with you. Jesus corrected them by saying, 'You aren't harmed by what you eat, but by what you think and say.' His friends didn't fully understand this because it was so different from what they'd been taught, so they asked him to explain it again.

Jesus told them, 'It is the thought-life that pollutes. For from within, out of men's hearts, come evil thoughts of lust, theft, murder ... wanting what belongs to others ... and all other folly. All these vile things come from within; they are what pollute you and make you unfit for God' (Mark 7:15,20–23, *The Living Bible*).

If it's true that our thought-life can be polluted so that we become 'unfit for God', then it's crucial that we keep our thought-life as cleaned up as possible. If we feed our minds with a diet of TV programmes and song lyrics that are full of violence, bad language and un-Godly attitudes, how can we hope to stay clean in our thinking and right with God? We wouldn't dream of washing our faces in a polluted stream, so why imagine that if we fill our heads with visual or verbal pollution we can be clean inside? It's much safer just to decide to stay clean and turn off the TV or hi-fi if what's on is a bit 'iffy'.

3 These first two points mean that we need to think carefully about the content of TV programmes, song lyrics or videos so we can be sure that we're not drinking in mental poison. The Bible gives us some more helpful advice in Philippians 4:8 (*The Living Bible*):

> Fix your thoughts on what is true and good and right. Think about things that are pure and lovely, and dwell on the fine, good things in others. Think about all you can praise God for and be glad about it.

So go on, put your favourite pop songs, TV programmes and films to the test.

Test 1 Do they focus on what is true, good and right – or do they concentrate on rebellion, deceit and doing wrong?

Test 2 Are they showing things that are pure and lovely – or are they smutty and crude, portraying the ugly side of life?

Test 3 Do they highlight the good in others – or do they glorify the 'downside' of human nature such as aggression, anger and hatred?

Test 4 Do they make you want to praise God – or do you feel kind of ashamed that God might know what

74

you've just watched or listened to?

These tests have nothing to do with what other people do, but have everything to do with what God says is good for us. *Eastenders* may be watched by twenty-one million people every week but that doesn't make it good – or bad. How popular it is, who recommends it and what time of the day it's on are not the guiding factors as far as God is concerned, but the four tests listed above *are* a useful guide to safe watching and listening.

SO WHAT?

1 Just because friends rave about a particular song, or a particular film gets a five-star rating in the *TV Times*, or a programme is on at the seemingly 'harmless' time of 6.00 pm, doesn't mean it's worth listening to or watching. Stand up for yourself and make your own decisions based on God's standards.

2 If your parents are Christians they are (hopefully) trying to guide you as to what is suitable for you to watch and listen to. Respect their wishes and be thankful that they love you enough to take the trouble to try to protect you from mental pollution.

3 Sometimes you won't know whether a programme is OK or a record passes the four tests listed above unless you actually watch or listen to it. If while you are watching or listening you start to feel it isn't the sort of thing that you should be tuning in to, then turn it off or, if other people in the family want to keep it on, leave the room and find something safer to do.

4 Some people will argue that TV programmes have to focus on the unpleasant side of life because for many people that's what life is like. They say that if every programme, soap opera and film was about the good, true and lovely then TV wouldn't be showing life as it really is for millions of people.

In one sense that's true. But just because life is hard for many people, and violence, swearing, pain or poverty are part of their everyday lives, it doesn't mean we have to sit down in front of a TV screen and be entertained by such things. It would be much better if we spent the time slumped in front of the screen actually helping or praying for people we know for whom life is tough.

5 Write down a list of your three favourite programmes and three favourite pop songs and run them through the four tests explained above. How do they do? Pass or fail? Any changes needed?

It'll be all right on the night

You may remember what I've told you before about Mr Grovey, our Drama teacher, but I haven't told you yet about the time Mr Grovey decided to put on a school play. Our school hasn't got a great tradition of dramatic productions, so this was to be a bit of a first. Mr Grovey chose something suitably dramatic called *Guns Across The Sea*.

The play was about an old hermit who lives in a barrel on the beach and who befriends a beautiful young woman, daughter of the local squire. Butler (the Hermit) had been an International Pogo Stick champion whose life took a turn for the worse when his spring broke in the 1962 World Championships. Sequin (the Beautiful Young Heiress) takes pity on Butler (the Ex-hopping Hermit), and cheers him up by visiting him and reading back issues of *Yellow Pages* to him. The Squire (Sequin's dad) is hopping mad that his delightful daughter is helping an Ex-hopping Hermit and goes out with a gun to blast Butler's barrel. Sequin secretly slips seaward and warns Butler, who escapes his barrel-

77

abode just before the Squire arrives and calls for him to come out with hands held heavenward. When no Hermit hurries out the Squire shouts a warning, counts to three and lets fly with both barrels, turning the Ex-hopping Hermit's home into a pile of splinters. The Squire is left harrassed and hopeless, whilst the play closes with Butler and Sequin escaping across the moors, holding hands and heading off into the night to start a new life as Husband and Wife.

There was obviously a lot more to it, but that's enough detail for you to understand the plot. Mr Grovey auditioned several people for the lead roles and Keith Cray got the part of Butler the Hermit, on the basis that he had the looks of a Pogo Stick Champion. Denise Smith was to be Sequin because she was a regular *Yellow Pages* reader in real life, and James Walker was to play the Squire because he was good at blowing things up (he once blew up his dad's garden shed with nothing but his chemistry set and a bottle of barbecue lighter fuel – impressive eh?).

With the characters all chosen, several weeks of rehearsals started and the play began to take shape. Keith got into the part so much that he claimed that he was sleeping in a barrel at home (although no one believed him). Denise practised so regularly that she had memorised the whole of *Yellow Pages* by the opening night. Perhaps the less said about James' preparation the better, except to note that the local fire brigade had their busiest time of the year in the two weeks leading up to the first night of the play.

So the great day arrived. Dress rehearsal in the morning, first performance to local junior schools in the afternoon and first public performance in the evening. The dress rehearsal went well, and in the afternoon

Keith claimed that he was sleeping in a barrel at home...

performance everyone remembered their lines, Keith looked suitably hermit-like and Denise read so beautifully that at least half of the audience were convinced that *Yellow Pages* was a previously unknown work by William Shakespeare!

Finally James' big moment arrived, and right on cue Darren Baron (Lighting, Sound and Special Effects) ignited the stage 'thunder flash' which gave the effect of the Squire's gun being fired and caused the barrel to disintegrate. It was very dramatic, and the flash and crash caused all the children from the junior schools to jump with surprise and fright. When the dust settled, Butler and Sequin were seen running hand in hand into the distance to start their new life together. A happy ending, and the whole thing was much appreciated by the assembled ranks of eight to eleven year olds.

The evening performance also started well, but this time things went badly wrong at James' big moment. James (alias the Squire) rushed onto the stage and saw the barrel from which Butler had just escaped. He approached it menacingly and thundered his lines, 'Come out you vile fellow. I'll teach you to sully my Sequin with your sordid suggestions. Come out I say. Don't think you can meddle with me, you half-witted Ex-hopping Hermit.'

No reply came from the empty barrel so the Squire, still thinking that Butler was inside, raised his shotgun to his shoulder and with his voice trembling with rage called out, 'I'm going to count to three and, if you don't come out, I'll blast you and your barrel to the other side of the ocean. One... Two... All right, don't say I didn't warn you... Three...'

James pulled the trigger and·... nothing. Absolutely nothing. No flash. No bang. No disintegrating barrel, just a long, embarrassed silence. The special effects had failed to go off. This had never happened before and James was completely thrown off course by it. He thought quickly. 'Should I shout out "bang, bang"?' he wondered. If only he had, he might have got away with it, but instead, in the split second that he had to think what to do, he decided to rerun the last few lines in case the special effects would work next time.

'OK, you were lucky that time – forgot to load the gun – but watch out now. I'm going to count to three and if you don't come out I'll blast you and your barrel to the other side of the ocean. One... Two.. All right, don't say I didn't warn you... Three...'

Sadly, nothing happened again. The problem with

the special effects 'thunder flash' was in the box hidden inside the barrel on stage and no one could get on to correct it. Unfortunately some members of the audience began to see the funny side of James' dilemma and a few muffled giggles could be heard in the hall.

'Just carry on!' hissed Mr Grovey from the wings of the stage, but stage fright had taken over and James seemed incapable of doing anything but rerunning the sequence yet again in the blind hope that this time it would surely work. His voice tight with emotion he almost screamed, 'OK, you were lucky that time, I had the gun round the wrong way – but watch out now. I'm going to count to three and if you don't come out I'll blast you and your barrel to the other side of the ocean. One... Two... All right, don't say I didn't warn you... Three...'

Again, deafening silence, ended this time not by a few polite giggles but by gales of side-splitting laughter from just about everyone in the audience who, despite trying very hard, were unable to contain their amusement. The trouble was that now James saw the funny side of it too, and he joined in the laughter on stage. This only served to encourage the audience to greater heights of merriment. In fact James laughed so much, he fell over onto the barrel which must have jogged the special effects box hidden inside. At that point it ignited with a huge 'crash, bang, wallop' leaving James slightly deafened but still rolling around the stage, crying with laughter.

There was really no point going on. A period drama had been turned into a one-man comedy turn. Mr Grovey instructed the curtains to be pulled across to bring the proceedings to an untimely end.

In the dressing room (actually a converted science

lab) afterwards Mr Grovey, looking rather unwell I thought, gave us a little talk along the lines of 'Never mind-we-can-only-do-our-best-and-it'll-be-all-right-tomorrow-night'. He ended by saying something quite unusual for him. He said, 'When you go to bed tonight, pray that everything will go OK tomorrow.' This was strange because Mr Grovey is not exactly the religious sort. I suppose the fact that he was asking us to pray shows just how much the events of the evening had unsettled him.

Anyway, I said a prayer that night. It went something like this: 'Dear God, thanks for a good laugh tonight. Please help tomorrow's show to be even funnier. Amen.'

THINKY BIT

Did you know that lots of surveys show that nearly everyone, at some time or another, says a prayer. In fact, more people claim to pray than actually claim to believe in God! (Think about that for a minute and you'll realise what a state some people are in – who are they praying to? !)

How about you? Do you pray? Do you find it easy to explain to your friends what prayer is and how it works? For lots of people a qustion like, 'You don't believe in prayer, do you?' would be a real Superglue Sandwich, especially if at the back of your mind you're thinking, 'Well, I do pray, but God doesn't seem to answer!' So let's take a look at what prayer is and how it does, and doesn't, work'.

PRAYERTIP 1 – *Nearly everyone prays but a Christian aims to pray like Jesus.*
As we've just seen, nearly everyone claims that, at some

time or another, they pray. Usually it's when, like Mr Grovey, they get to a disaster or some situation which makes them frightened or feel that they can't cope. Nearly all the world's major religions encourage their followers to pray to their gods. In fact, it's possible that praying is one of the most common activities in the world (although clearly people in other religions won't be talking to Jesus when they pray).

For a Christian, praying is supposed to be more than a panic reaction to being in trouble. Christians are followers of Jesus, so it's worth looking at the way Jesus prayed and talked about prayer so that we can learn more for ourselves.

PRAYERTIP 2 – *When you pray, try to find somewhere quiet.*
Jesus thought prayer was so important that quite often he would stay up all night to pray. How does your prayer life compare with that? Prayer for Jesus wasn't just taking a Christmas list of 'wants' to God. When Jesus prayed, he deliberately went somewhere that he could be quiet, and not only talk to God but also spend time thinking about what God wanted, without the distractions caused by other people. It's not surprising then that Jesus taught his friends to pray in a quiet place. This is what he said: 'When you pray, go to your room, close the door, and pray to your Father, who is unseen. And your Father, who sees what you do in private, will reward you' (Matthew 6:6).

Of course you can send up a quick prayer anywhere, but that should never be *instead of* a proper prayer session with God in the quiet of your own room (or wherever you can find some peace and quiet).

PRAYERTIP 3 – *Prayer is a simple conversation between you and God, not a religious speech from you to God.*
Have you ever heard adults who seem to talk to God in a different voice to the one that they use for talking to everyone else? Maybe not, but it can be hard to talk to God in a natural sort of way, simply because he *is* God and maybe we feel that we need to impress him. That's not true.

Jesus told people off when they used long words and posh phrases to try to impress God with their prayers. He told his followers to keep it simple and just say what they wanted to: 'When you pray, do not use a lot of meaningless words, as the pagans do, who think that God will hear them because their prayers are long. Do not be like them' (Matthew 6:7).

PRAYERTIP 4 – *Use Jesus' prayer as a pattern for yours.*
When I was ten I prayed nearly every day that I would get a Scalextric for Christmas. I really, really wanted one and I thought that prayer was a way of making God give me what I wanted. In fact, nearly all my prayers then were asking God for things that *I* wanted. I never stopped to think how God felt about that.

Imagine for a moment that you have a good friend who you really get on well with. If, one day, that person spent the whole day just telling you what they wanted, you might find it a bit off. If the next day was the same, and the next day, and so on, it wouldn't be long before you began to find a way to avoid them. Far from being a good friend they've become a selfish, greedy person!

Prayer-like-Jesus-prayed has many different parts to it. Most of them are summed up in a prayer which Jesus taught to his friends. He said, 'This then, is how you should pray':

> Our Father in heaven: may your holy name be
> honoured;

It's always best to start praying by remembering how
big and special God is. If you don't think God is very
big, you won't be able to pray very big prayers!

> May your Kingdom come;
> May your will be done on earth as it is in heaven.

Here's the *great* secret of prayer that many people never
discover. Prayer isn't asking for what *I* want; it's
working out what *God* wants and asking for that. Of
course, I might want exactly what God wants. But there
might be a huge difference between the two things, so
I need to be ready to change what I want to be the
same as what God wants. This is why prayer needs
to include time when we *think*, and read our Bible, to
discover what God wants. This is what people mean
when they talk about 'listening' to God.

> Give us today the food we need.

Only now, after thinking about what God wants, can
we pray for what we *need*. Notice Jesus didn't say, 'Pray
for your daily Scalextric'! God promises to supply our
'needs' not our 'wants'. It's also good to be praying for
other people's needs, too, so that our prayer life doesn't
get too self-centred.

> Forgive us the wrongs that we have done,
> as we forgive the wrongs
> that others have done to us.

85

Sometimes we can be very hurt by things that other people do and say to us. We can also hurt other people in just the same way. These hurts get in the way of our friendship with God and prayer is the way to get rid of them. Saying 'sorry' for the wrong things we have done, and telling God that we forgive people who have hurt us, results in God wiping the slate clean and helping us deal with our problems. It's quite helpful to be specific – rather than just say 'I'm sorry for anything I've done wrong', say 'Jesus, I'm sorry for being rude to Rebecca today. I know what I said was unkind and upset her and I'm sorry. Please forgive me.' (This prayer only makes sense if you have actually been rude to someone called Rebecca today, but you know what I mean! !) Or rather than saying 'I forgive anyone who has hurt me today', it's better to get real and say 'I found it really upsetting when Mum blamed me for dropping that cup. Lord, you know it was an accident. I know Mum was tired and probably didn't mean to be so angry. I forgive her now. Please help her to forgive me.' (When you say sorry to God, it would be good to apologise to the person you've upset too.)

> Do not bring us to hard testing,
> but keep us safe from the Evil One.

Finally in Jesus' model prayer, he taught his followers to pray for safety from God's enemy, Satan. Sadly, we are surrounded by evil, but the Good News is that our God is stronger than all the evil in the world put together! Praying for his protection for ourselves, our families and friends is an important part of our daily prayer times.

Jesus never expected us to repeat the words of his prayer as though they were some kind of magical spell, but rather he meant us to use his prayer as an example of how we might organise our prayers.

So here's Jesus' prayer summarised under five headings. You could use these with your own words in your personal prayer time.

PRAISE God and think of his bigness.

THINK about what God wants done in the things you are praying for (it may help to read the Bible too at this stage).

ASK for your needs and the needs of others.

ADMIT things that you need forgiving for and tell God that you have forgiven others.

PRAY for protection from evil.

PRAYERTIP 5 – *Keep praying and don't give up.*
The last point to remember about prayer is that we need to keep on praying. Jesus told a story about a dishonest judge who refused to help a poor widow. Day after day she would come to his courtroom and ask for justice, but he couldn't be bothered to do anything to help her. However, eventually he got so fed up with her constant nagging that he decided to give her her rights. Jesus said that if a bad, dishonest judge can be moved to action by someone who keeps on and on asking, surely a good God will be quick to answer the constant prayers of his people. The point of this story was 'to teach them (his disciples) that they should

always pray and never become discouraged' (Luke 18:1).

Maybe there are things that you have prayed about in the past and have given up on now. Well, if you think that you were praying selfishly, asking God for the wrong things, then maybe it's a good thing that you *have* stopped. But if you are sure that what you were praying for is what God would want, then start praying again. Keep on at God until you get an answer (even if that answer isn't what you expect!).

SO WHAT?

1 You can take confidence from the fact that, even if your friends don't think praying is very important, Jesus thought it was top priority. After all who knows most about prayer, your mates or Jesus?

2 When friends say that they don't believe in prayer you can ask them why and maybe explain a bit about real prayer using some of the information in this chapter.

3 You can try to put these five Prayertips into action. Why not keep a Prayerlog – a special notebook where you write down things you want to keep on praying for, and where you write down when God answers!

4 It's encouraging that although prayer is so vital, it's so simple. Anyone can do it! No posh words needed, no dressing up or visiting a church building – just you and God in private.

Le grand mistake

Learning a foreign language is something you can't get out of at our school. It doesn't seem to matter whether or not you ever intend to go abroad, or even whether or not you can speak proper English yet, you still have to learn a foreign language. For me that meant French, twice a week with Mrs Rolands who only spoke to us in French – whether we understood it or not! Last Tuesday she greeted us with her customary, 'Bonjour, la classe.'

'Bonjour, Madame Rolands,' we duly replied. Just about everyone in the class could cope with this bit of ritual.

'Ca va? (All well?)' she continued.

'Ca va bien, merci (All well, thank you),' we replied. We always said that all was well whether or not it was really true since we had never been taught how to say, 'No, I've got a thumping headache, it's pouring with rain and my gerbil died last night' in French.

'Bon! Aujourd-hui, nous allons faire un petit test de

We always said that all was well whether or not it really was. . .

vocabulaire.'

Oh no, I'd forgotten that today was our vocabulary test. My mind whirred back over the last twenty-four hours to see how I could have made such a mistake. Oh yes. There had been so much else to remember last night – TV to watch, new Sega game to master, Subbuteo tournament to finish. No wonder I hadn't managed to squeeze in any French revision with that lot on my mind. Ah well, now what did we do last lesson. . .

I was brought back to the present by the fact that Madame Roland was talking again (en français, of course!) and, worse still, she seemed to be speaking to me personally.

'Attention, David. Tu reves de quelquechose? Si tu es fatigué il faut que tu te couches de bonne heure, n'est-ce pas?'

I didn't quite get all that, but I think a loose translation would be, 'Stop sitting there looking like a corpse on strike, get your pen out and get ready to start the test.' That's what I did anyway and it seemed to satisfy Madame R.

'Bon. Il y a dix questions. Je vais ecrire dix mots en anglais sur le tableau noir; vous allez copier les mots et vous allez les traduire en français,' she explained.

Not so bad, I suppose. Ten English words to copy down from the board onto our pieces of paper. All we had to do then was put the equivalent French word next to each.

To cut a boring test short, here's my finished article. English word given by Madame Roland on the left followed by my translation into French on the right. Bet you're impressed.

1	The car	Le renault
2	The car driver	Le Alain Prost
3	The garage	La maison de renault
4	The greengrocer	L'homme de veggie
5	The aeroplane	La concorde
6	The sun	Le news papier anglais
7	The hamburger	Le grand mac
8	The Italian restaurant	Le pizza hut
9	The ice cream	La cornetto
10	The station	La rage

In all honesty I had struggled a bit, especially with questions 1 to 9. However, I felt that I'd finished on a triumphant note because I'd eventually remembered doing all about railway stations last lesson. 'The station – la rage'. Yup, I was sure. We handed in our tests and the lesson continued to its conclusion.

A week passed before we all sat in Madame Roland's class again, awaiting the return of our marked tests with varying degrees of hopeful anticipation or descending doom. I was firmly in the latter category. I'd looked up some of the words that we'd had in the test in my French dictionary and it didn't seem that I'd done too well, but I would soon know for sure.

The opening pleasantries being over, Madame Roland produced the pile of marked tests and announced that everyone had done well (my spirits lifted). Everyone that is, except (my spirits sank) David.

'Zero! Zero! ! Pas un seul point,' she accused.

What? Not a single mark? She must have made a mistake. What about question 10, 'station – la rage'. I was sure I'd got that right. In fact, I was so sure that I tried to explain.

'Je m'excuse, Madame Roland, but je believe vous avez made une erreur,' I blurted.

'Comment, David?' she looked taken aback at my sudden fluency in French.

I explained about 'la rage'. She explained it was no good having all the right letters if you didn't manage to get them in the right order!

' "Station" c'est "la gare", pas "la rage". G – A – R – E, pas R – A – G – E,' she slowly explained.

I was horrified by my own stupidity, but my sense of justice made me speak up just once more. After all, I *had* got all the right letters and it *was* only the order that was wrong. Surely I deserved half a mark at least. I plucked up my courage, and most of my French

92

vocabulary, and said. 'Madame, s'il vous plait? Can je have un half point pour aving les lettres correct?'

Madame Roland's reply was lengthy and belligerent. I've no idea exactly what she said but, judging from her tone of voice, her answer was a very drawn out French way of saying 'No'.

So there you are. Zero for French. Spelling just isn't fair, is it? I think there ought to be loads of ways of spelling any word – as long as you get all the right letters in. I mean, what does it really matter?

THINKY BIT

Of course it's daft to think that there can be several ways of spelling a word. Even if you have all the right letters, there is still a right and a wrong way to order them. Ot od ti ayn ohrte awy would jsut deal ot consofiun (if you see what I mean).

There are people, however, who apply similar ideas to religion. They say that as long as, more or less, the right ideas are there, you can believe what you want. So as long as there's an idea of God, of worship, of doing what is right and ignoring what is evil, all religions are just about the same. Some churches even have special services where people from different religions take part, as though there was no difference between them. But are they really all worshipping and serving the same God?

No! This idea is dangerously wrong. It's as confused as the idea that, as long as you have all the right letters in a word, you can spell it how you want. The truth is that all the world's religions are different, and Christianity is not just another way of putting a selection of different religious ideas together.

You may have friends at school who belong to a

different religion and maybe you've wondered what they believe. Maybe they have asked *you* what you believe and how it is different to what they believe. That question can be a real Superglue Sandwich if you're not ready for it. Here's a quick look at some of the differences between Christianity and four other major world religions. (There's a lot more to know about these religions, so if you want to know more about any one in particular – maybe because you have a friend who belongs to one – ask your youth leader or church leader to help you get some more information.)

Judaism is the name given to the religion of Jewish people. They believe in one God who is written about in their holy book or Scriptures. Their Scriptures are exactly the same as the Old Testament part of your Bible, but they don't believe that the New Testament should be accepted as a part of God's holy book. Christians also believe in one God who is written about in a holy book (the Bible), but we believe that the New Testament and its accounts of Jesus are a vital part of God's book.

The first five books of the Jewish Scriptures are especially honoured by Jewish people, and the Law written in those books (summed up in the Ten Commandments) must be kept if a Jew is to be accepted by God. Christians believe that we become friends with God when we believe that Jesus died to save us from our sins and when we accept Jesus as our King, not when we manage to keep a list of laws.

The Jews believe that Moses was the greatest prophet who ever lived. Christians believe that Jesus was the greatest prophet who ever lived.

Jews don't believe that Jesus was God living as a

man on earth. Christians, on the other hand, do believe that Jesus was God-in-a-body, because that's what the Bible means when it says, 'For in Christ there is all of God in a human body' (Colossians 2:9, *The Living Bible*).

Islam is the name given to the religion of Muslim people. They too have a holy book called the Qur'an. They believe that it was written in heaven by their god (called Allah) and that he revealed it to the prophet Muhammad by means of the Archangel Gabriel. Christians believe that their holy book, the Bible, was written by many ordinary men who were inspired by God to write down what he wanted.

Muslims regard Muhammad, who lived about six hundred years after Jesus, as the greatest prophet and apostle of Allah. Christians believe that Jesus was the greatest prophet of God.

Muslims believe that when they die they will be judged for everything they have done. All the good will be put on one side of the scales and all the bad on the other. If there's enough good the scales will tip and Allah may allow them to enter Paradise. (The only exception to this is if a Muslim dies fighting in a 'holy war'. Then he believes that he will automatically enter Paradise.) Christians believe that we are given eternal life with God as a free gift when we put our trust in Jesus. We don't have to earn it. The Bible says, 'Being saved is a gift; if a person could earn it by doing good, then it wouldn't be free – but it is! It is *given* to those who do *not* work for it. 'For God declares sinners to be good in his sight if they have faith in Christ to save them from God's wrath' (Romans 4:4,5, *The Living Bible*).

Hinduism is the name given to a variety of religions that come from the country of India. Hindus believe in many gods. If you have ever seen pictures of an Indian temple on television you will perhaps have noticed the many little statues or idols, each representing a Hindu god. Christians believe in one God who we know through the Bible and who is in control of the whole universe, not millions of little gods each with their own area of responsibility.

Hindus believe in many different ways of getting to know their gods. They would have no trouble in accepting Jesus as *a* prophet, but they could only accept him as *one of the many* prophets that they believe in.

The Bible, on the other hand, says that not only is there only *one* God, but there is only *one* way to know him: 'Salvation is to be found through him (Jesus) alone; in all the world there is no one else whom God has given who can save us' (Acts 4:12). Even Jesus himself said, 'I am the Way – yes, and the Truth and the Life. No one can get to the Father except by means of me' (John 14:7, *The Living Bible*).

Hindus believe that when you die you are reborn again, as something or someone else. This idea is called 'reincarnation' (there's a big word to impress your teachers with!). If you're good in this life you'll be reborn as a better grade of being in the next life, but if you have been a bad person you'll return in your next life as a *lower* life-form, like a slug (or an Arsenal supporter!). Christians believe that we only live once on this earth, and when we die we are judged according to whether or not we are friends of Jesus. 'Everyone must die once, and after that be judged by God' (Hebrews 9:27).

Buddhism is the name of the religion given to the followers of Buddha, a religious teacher who lived in the North of India about six hundred years before Jesus was born. (This means that he was around at about the same time as the Old Testament prophet, Ezekiel.) Buddhists don't believe in a god of any sort. They don't worship Buddha as a god, but hold his teaching in the highest regard. It hardly needs pointing out that there's immediately a difference with Christians who believe in the existence of God!

Buddhists don't believe that life has a beginning or an end. A bit like Hindus (see above), they believe that life is a kind of wheel that just keeps taking you round and round through different phases of existence. Christians do believe that life on earth started when God decided to create it ('In the beginning . . . God created the universe' Genesis 1:1) and that one day it will all end. We also believe that our lives *on this earth* had a beginning and one day will have a definite ending.

The ultimate goal of existence for a Buddhist is to become released from the world with all its suffering and struggle, and to become nothing or 'Nirvana' which is a kind of cosmic black hole which Buddhists hope will one day swallow them up. Christians, far from hoping to be swallowed up into nothingness, hope and believe that they will live for ever with God. As Christians we have already begun new lives that will last for ever – even beyond our physical death. 'For God loved the world so much that he gave his only Son, so that everyone who believes in him may not die but have eternal life' (John 3:16).

You can see from this brief look at four of the world's major religions that the idea that all religions are the same, and that we're all worshipping the same God and walking the same religious pathway, is nonsense. There are just too many big differences between us to allow us to believe that we're simply different parts of the same thing.

It isn't possible to explain everything about these four religions in such a short chapter, nor even to begin to mention the many other religions which exist in the world. But I hope you're beginning to understand that, even though there are some things that are the same between Christianity and other faiths, there is something special, something absolutely unique about Christianity. If somebody suggests to you that all religions are the same, perhaps you can now un-gum your lips and explain one or two ways that they're different. Or at least offer to lend them this book to help them see things more clearly! !

SO WHAT?

1 If at school (or even at church) people try to convince you that Muslims, Hindus, Jews, Buddhists and Christians can worship together (say, in assembly) because they're all worshipping the same God, you now know that it's impossible. You cannot worship your God by taking part in a Hindu festival or by saying Muslim prayers.

2 All of this does *not* mean, however, that people of other religions are our enemies! ! God loves all people (even though all people don't love him!) and God wants us to show his love to people of every race and religion. So jokes about people of other religions, name-calling, or any other form of disrespect, are wrong and not what Jesus wants from his followers.

3 You will have noticed that Christians don't disagree with everything that other religions teach. There are some things that we would broadly agree with, say, in Judaism or Islam. It's usually more helpful when talking to people from other faiths to start with the things that we share rather than trying to 'prove them wrong' on the things where we differ.

4 If we want to talk to someone of another religion about what we believe, it's important to find out as much as possible about their faith first, so that we don't unnecessarily offend them.

5 If you feel that you *can't* talk about your faith, by far the most powerful form of witness for Jesus is for you to be as kind and generous as possible to your friends of other faiths.

6 A big difference between Christianity and nearly every other religion is our different understanding of who Jesus is. As we have seen, many other religions emphasise *some* of the things that we believe about Jesus, but none of them believe that he was God-in-a-body. To talk about Jesus you need to be as clued up as possible about him. Try and read a bit from one of the four Gospels every day so that you're continually topping up your knowledge of who Jesus was and what he said and did.

7 Another big difference between Christianity and other religions is that in other religions we humans must work hard to make ourselves good enough for God. Christians believe that we can't earn God's friendship by being clever or generous, by praying hard or reading our Bibles, but that God chooses to give us the gift of his friendship. All we have to do is accept that gift. This should blow our minds!

Reports of pain

The end of a school term is mostly good news. After a tough sixteen weeks of term the prospect of staying in bed until lunch time each day is very appealing. However, there's one major obstacle to end-of-term bliss; it's the end-of-term report.

The end-of-term report is your teachers' chance to get even with you. Teachers, who have been more or less polite to you all term, suddenly get offensive and drag into the open things that you had forgotten – or that you thought they had never noticed – and things which you certainly didn't want your parents to know about.

Despite its obvious shortcomings, the school report system has always been accepted as an inevitable part of suffering school. Until, that is, Matthew Brady brilliantly spotted a great injustice built into the usual way of doing things and set about putting things right. The flaw Matthew noticed was that whereas teachers were always allowed, even encouraged, to write nasty things home about us, we were never allowed to do the same about our teachers! The more he thought about it, the more the unfairness of this way of carrying on offended Matthew's sense of right and wrong. So he called a secret class meeting behind the gym at break time.

About twelve of us bothered to turn up at the meeting. (We later found out that this was because Matthew had kept the meeting so secret, no one else in the class knew about it!) Matthew explained his suggested improvements to the school's report system.

'It just ain't fair that Mr Kent can write to my mum and tell her that I failed to hand in seven lots of homework, when I can't write to his wife and tell her that *he* failed to mark three of our seven maths tests,' Matthew explained. We murmured our agreement as the full enormity of the injustice began to bear in on us.

'Yeah, that's right! And when Mrs Taylor said that my spelling could be improved, my dad gave me spelling tests every day of the Christmas holidays. But it was her that stuck up the "English Cuboard" notice with no "p" in cupboard. I bet if her husband knew he'd be furious,' joined in Kelly Chavra.

'Right! Well, what I reckon we should do is to find out our teachers' addresses and send home end-of-term reports for them,' concluded Matthew. The scheme was bold, but nonetheless it was the only way of putting right what was clearly an unfair situation. Everyone was sworn to secrecy and Matthew began to give out jobs to different people in order to put the plan into action.

Matthew himself would prepare A4 sheets of paper and pass them around the class and each person would write a comment about the teacher whose name appeared at the top of the paper. When everyone had

had a chance to write a comment on every teacher's piece of paper, Kelly would collect them and put them in envelopes. In the meantime, several other class members were detailed to find out where each teacher lived and to pass their address back to Kelly.

The main task for the rest of us was to write a short comment about each of our teachers, summing up their ability, behaviour and application to their job (this, after all is what they did for us). I enjoyed this bit and here, just for the record, is a selection of my comments:

'Mr Kent's intellect has all the cutting edge of an apricot flan although he does know some good jokes.'

'Mrs Burton's punkshuality is not good and also she is rather late quite often sometimes.' (I got a bit confused with that one but I think her husband will get the point.)

'If Mr Grovey put as much effort into his lesson preparation as he does into drinking coffee the class would all be a lot more cleverer.'

'I think it was quite unfair of Mr Stevens to throw me out of his science lesson – I didn't mean to blow up Brian Smart's pencil case, I only meant to singe it a little bit.'

'Ms Brubeck is always very nice to me and she has nice teeth.'

'Mrs Blakency is probably the oldest teacher in the school and she is very strict. My grandma used to say "If your face wants to smile let it and if it doesn't want to smile, make it", and I think Mrs Blakeney would do well to take my grandma's advice.'

There was lots more, some good, some bad, but all very honest!

To our surprise our plan went fairly smoothly. At least it did until Kelly Chavra was away ill and I got lumbered with the job of collecting all the teachers' reports together, checking everyone's comments for spelling mistakes (yes, *me* checking for spelling errors!) and putting each report into an envelope for posting. Due to the great secrecy which surrounded our plan I obviously couldn't do this work at school so I took all the reports home and in the evening laid them out in the privacy of my bedroom to check them through.

I was right in the middle of this mammoth task when I remembered that I hadn't set the video for the live Match on TV, so I dashed down to set it before my little brother could set it to record tomorrow's edition of *Sesame Street*. When I returned to my bedroom (having spent five minutes or so in the kitchen relieving the biscuit tin of some of its contents) I was horrified to find Dad standing in the middle of my bedroom carefully reading Mr Grovey's end-of-term report!

I was so shocked that I wished the floor would swallow me up – actually I thought that my wish had come true because in my anxiety I tripped over my school bag and landed in a pile at Dad's feet.

'What's this, then?'

Have you noticed how adults only ask you questions to which they already know the answer? I was trapped. Matthew's brilliant scheme (did I really think it was brilliant?) suddenly seemed about as sensible as throw-

I landed in a pile at Dad's feet.

ing tomatoes at an electric fan. If I confessed, I was in trouble and if I lied, I was in even bigger trouble. Well, my conscience won and I told the truth. It was amazing how the very same arguments that sounded so convincing behind the gym two weeks ago could sound so feeble now.

Having heard the evidence and asked a few extra questions Dad suggested that I should destroy all the reports that my class mates had written and have nothing more to do with the plan. As punishment for getting involved in the first place I was going to lose two weeks' pocket money. But I knew the real punishment would come at school tomorrow when I had to tell everyone what had happened. I could just hear them now.

'You stupid wally! Fancy leaving them lying about in public – you were just asking for trouble.'

'All that slog for nothing.'

'Yeah, thanks very much. I bet your dad tells my dad and I get grief from him. You're a brick-brain; what are you?'

And on and on they'd go in similar vein. To be honest the prospect of suffering the wrath of my friends didn't appeal too much (strange, eh? ?) and I didn't know if I had the guts to go into school tomorrow. I certainly didn't sleep much that night.

THINKY BIT

Nobody enjoys suffering – it's a well-known fact! We'd all sooner live in a world where nothing ever went wrong, no one ever got hurt and the good guys always won in the end. The fact that the world is *not* like that is pretty obvious and it makes us face the tough question, 'How can there be so much suffering and pain in the world when it's supposed to have been well made by a good God?' Did he get it wrong? Is he too weak to sort out the mess? Doesn't he care? Maybe you've never thought about these questions, but sooner or later you'll have to, because for many people – probably including many of your friends – they are the very problems that stop them believing in a God who is good. Here are some ideas to help you get between the crusts of these particular Superglue Sandwiches.

1 *Pain is good for you!*
What? No, don't shut the book, I haven't flipped – it really is! Pain is the body's way of telling us that something's wrong. If I pick up something that's too

hot, my hand quickly phones my brain and says 'Quick! Drop it! !' – and, without thinking, I do. If it didn't hurt when I picked up something hot, I could seriously damage my skin, nerves and whole hand and arm. The pain warning has been good for me.

Similarly if I get too tired I might start to get lots of headaches. If I go to the doctor she might say, 'You need to get more sleep and stop working so late at night'. The pain, which I didn't enjoy, sent me to the doctor who was able to diagnose the problem and prevent further damage being caused by my overwork. Once again, the pain warning has done me good.

In this sense, then, it's true that 'pain is good for you', but clearly not all pain and suffering is good and useful. What about when we get ill and the illness seems to drag on and on? It's a fact that our bodies are not indestructible; they break down and sometimes, sadly, no repair is possible. Jesus met lots of people who had long-term illnesses and, if they asked, he would always pray that they would get better – and when Jesus prayed they always did! We too can pray for other people who are unwell, and sometimes God will heal them – but at other times nothing seems to change. At times like these it's helpful to remember two things:

(a) We should still go on showing the person God's love by caring for them in whatever way possible. Jesus said that looking after a sick person is like looking after him (Matthew 25:36).

(b) One day God will make them completely well, either in this life or in the new life that he has promised his friends after they die.

But it's not only understanding our own aches and pains that causes us difficulties. What about tragedies and disasters, wars and famines? OK. That leads us on to our next point.

2 Danger, Men at Work!

You may have seen this sentence on a road sign warning you, for example, to watch out because you're about to ride your bike down a metre deep hole left by the local Gas company! Imagine that you ignored the warning sign and cycled into the hole. When you came round in hospital, who would be to blame for your suffering? Any honest answer would surely have to be either 'the local Gas company', 'the man who dug the hole' or 'the silly cyclist who ignored the warning sign'! It would be unfair to blame God since he didn't dig the hole or push you down it.

A lot of the suffering in the world is caused by people. In 1987 there was a terrible disaster when a cross-channel ferry sank whilst leaving the Belgian port of Zeebrugge. Many people were killed and the next day, as the terrible facts were becoming clearer – but before anyone knew exactly what had happened – a national newspaper printed a picture of the overturned boat with the caption, 'And they say that God is good!' The newspaper reporter needed someone to blame, so he blamed God. But, if God is really in control of every single boat crossing the English channel, surely newspapers should also print stories saying how good he is in ensuring that there are thousands of safe crossings every year! !

When the facts became clearer it was revealed that the ferry sank because a crew member had failed to close the huge bow-doors at the front of the ferry, allow-ing water to enter and capsize the ship. A case perhaps of 'Danger, Man *Not* At Work'.

Many so-called 'natural' disasters are caused, or made worse, by humans. Despite the fact that we're told that the earth can produce enough food to feed everyone on the planet, many die of starvation because some countries are too greedy to share the food out evenly, and some governments would sooner spend their money on weapons of war than food for their people. *God* has provided enough food, but *humans* haven't shared it round fairly.

Tokyo, one of the world's largest cities, is built in an area where the experts know there's a major earthquake about every seventy years. When the earthquake comes and buildings fall and people are killed, would it be fair to blame God? Surely the blame should rest with those who allowed this major city to be developed in what is known to be a dangerous place.

To blame God wouldn't be fair, any more than it would be fair to blame him if you get toothache because you've eaten too many sweets. We must admit that the choices we make can cause us to suffer. In many cases of suffering in the world it is humans that are the problem, not God.

3 *Enemy action*

So how did the world that God looked at and said was 'very good' (Genesis 1:31) get to the state where pain and suffering existed at all? The Bible lets us in on the secret, and it is that God has a powerful enemy who wants the exact opposite of everything that God wants. His name is Satan (which means 'deceiver') and he hates everything that God loves and tries to destroy everything that God creates.

Jesus put it like this: 'The thief (Satan) comes only in order to steal, to kill and to destroy. I have come in order that you might have life ... in all its fullness' (John 10:10). If Satan can steal happiness he will; if he can destroy health, he will; if he can kill our faith in God, he will. But remember, Satan is not as powerful as God and Jesus proved this when, time after time, he destroyed the work of Satan in the world that he lived in.

Jesus' life on earth was a kind of battle against the suffering that God hates and which Satan loves. When Jesus saw a person suffering with illness, he went into battle and made them better. When Jesus saw the forces of nature about to cause a 'natural disaster' and sink the boat he was in, he took control and told the wind and waves to settle down, and they did. When Jesus saw some of his best friends suffering grief because their brother, Lazarus, had died, he took pity on them and brought him back to life. When Jesus was faced with five thousand men suffering hunger, he fed them. John put it like this: 'The Son of God (Jesus) came to destroy these works of the devil' (1 John 3:8, *The Living Bible*).

More than that, Jesus came to tell us, and show us, what life will one day be like when all suffering is done away with. He said that for everyone who follows him God will make a new earth, where no suffering, sickness of any kind or evil will be allowed at all. John describes what it will be like in Revelation 21:1–5.

The evil in the world does cause suffering, and for a while God allows it, because he's waiting for as many people as possible to become Christians before he puts a stop to everything, by sending Jesus back to earth to start a new world for those who love him. Satan, and everyone who has chosen to ignore God in this life, will not be allowed into the new earth. Suffering will be a thing of the past. Living in a suffering world isn't pleasant, but the promise of God's defeat of his enemies and a new world, where only what he wants will happen, should give us hope for the future and encouragement to keep going through tough times.

SO WHAT?

1 If our friends blame God for all the bad things in the world we can now remember that some pain is good for us, that people, not God, have caused a lot of the suffering, and that God isn't happy with suffering and will one day put an end to it.

2 When we see someone suffering, we can be like Jesus and try to help them or pray for them. Like Jesus we can stand up for right and for people who aren't strong enough to look after themselves.

3 As we get older we can work for a better world where God's resources are shared fairly. This will mean not being greedy or selfish in the way that we live, and remembering that the more we take for ourselves, the less there is for other people to have.

4 When the going gets *really* tough, we can encourage ourselves by looking at God's promises about the future world that he's going to create for those who love him. Try looking up these verses. Think what it'll be like to live in such a world: Micah 4:3,4, Isaiah 11:6–9, Revelation 21:3–5.